Lift Up Your Hearts

A Pastoral, Theological,
and Historical Survey
of the Third Typical Edition
of *The Roman Missal*

EDITED BY

Reverend Robert L. Tuzik, STL, PHD

WITH A PREFACE BY

Francis Cardinal George, OMI

LITURGY
TRAINING
PUBLICATIONS

Nihil Obstat
Francis Cardinal George, OMI
Archdiocese of Chicago
December 20, 2010

Imprimatur
Francis Cardinal George, OMI
Archdiocese of Chicago
December 20, 2010

The *Nihil Obstat* and *Imprimatur* are declarations that the material is free from doctrinal or moral error and thus is granted permission to publish in accordance with c. 827. No legal responsibility is assumed by the grant of this permission. No implication is contained therein that those who have granted the *Nihil Obstat* and *Imprimatur* agree with the content, opinions, or statements expressed.

Library of Congress Control Number: 2011926088

ISBN 978-1-56854-922-4
LYH

Contents

Preface

Dear Friends in Christ:

Many years were spent preparing the translation of the third typical edition of *The Roman Missal*. In fact, this is the first major liturgical book to be issued since March 28, 2001, when the Congregation for Divine Worship and the Discipline of the Sacraments (CDWDS) issued *Liturgiam authenticam: On the Use of Vernacular Languages in the Publication of Books of the Roman Liturgy.*

The creation of the third typical edition of *The Roman Missal* involved consultations with clergy and laity from across the English speaking world. All of the Episcopal Conferences that are part of the International Commission on English in the Liturgy (ICEL) were consulted. The bishops who make up these conferences were encouraged to seek feedback from their clergy and laity and to make recommendations for changes to the proposed text that we submitted to them.

The Episcopal Board of ICEL under the leadership of Bishop Arthur Roche, Bishop of Leeds, England, worked tirelessly with the Bishops' Committee on Divine Worship (BCDW) under the leadership of Bishop Arthur Serratelli, chairman of the BCDW, to produce a translation that reflected the input of the various Bishops' Conferences that would use the third typical edition of *The Roman Missal*. The Episcopal Board and the BCDW prepared the final version of the translation that was approved by the Episcopal Conferences that make up ICEL and was submitted to the CDWDS in Rome.

When Pope John Paul II named me a Cardinal on January 18, 1998, I was appointed to be a member of the CDWDS, which would eventually produce in 2001 the revised norms for translating *The Roman Missal* into the vernacular, *Liturgiam authenticam*, and be responsible for reviewing and amending the proposed translation prior to sending it to the Holy Father for approval.

On July 19, 2001, I was appointed a member of the Vox Clara Committee of the CDWDS. Vox Clara was founded to advise the CDWDS on the English translation of liturgical texts and to strengthen the effective communication of the Holy See with the

Conferences of Bishops. I have found the meetings of Vox Clara to be a positive source of encouragement and assistance, improving the English translations submitted by the Conferences in the light of current norms for translation as well as involving the Episcopal Conferences in the dialogue leading up to final approval of a proposed translation for *The Roman Missal.*

From 1997 to 2006 I served as the USCCB Representative to ICEL. In this capacity, I had the opportunity to review every text that ICEL proposed during this period for approval and/or emendation by the Episcopal Conferences of ICEL. In addition, from 2001–2004 I served as chairman of the Bishops' Committee on the Liturgy, now called Bishops' Committee on Divine Worship. Consequently, I had the opportunity to review the texts of the revised edition of *The Roman Missal* from many different perspectives.

While no translation is perfect, I do believe that most people will find the translation of the liturgical texts in the third typical edition of *The Roman Missal* to be an improvement over the texts we had previously been using. It is important to remember that the norms under which the previous translation were composed and approved were different from the norms we currently have in place. After using the former texts for almost 40 years, we now have a better idea of what are qualities and values of the Roman tradition of prayer that we want to preserve in our English translation.

While you will find some authors in this book of essays criticizing the previous translation, you must not forget that many people are fond of the prayers that we have used for almost 40 years. It is my hope that by studying the history of the translation process and the rationale behind the improvements in the English translation, people will come to appreciate the virtues of the English translation now found in the third typical edition of *The Roman Missal.*

If people approach the revised edition with an open mind, I believe there will be many things that people will like about *The Roman Missal*:

- a more accurate translation of the Latin text
- greater attention to the poetry, rhyme, and rhythm of the liturgical text
- more obvious connections to the biblical and patristic sources of the liturgical text

- greater attention to the ability to sing the presidential prayers and the Preface
- new Masses for recently canonized saints
- addition of formerly approved Masses for Mary into the third typical edition of *The Roman Missal* (these Masses were previously released in a separate book)
- new Eucharistic Prayers.

I realize that some people find change difficult. On the other hand, the workshops on the revised Order of Mass that we have offered in the Archdiocese of Chicago have provided feedback from our laity that the changes in the people's parts are relatively minor. Most people tell us that they will adjust to these changes fairly quickly. In fact, they tend to be very positive about the changes and are looking forward to the use of the revised Missal.

Our priests will have a harder time adjusting to the new translation. Their parts are significantly different in wording, rhythm, and length. I have found that by following the format of the prayer printed on the page, reading sense units, pausing at commas and stopping at periods, proclaiming or singing the texts is fairly easy. I ask our priests to be patient and to take a positive approach to presenting the third typical edition of *The Roman Missal* to their people. After all is said and done, the positive reception of and effective use of the revised edition of *The Roman Missal* will depend on liturgical leadership in parishes, institutions, and religious communities.

The BCDW, ICEL, the Liturgical Institute at Mundelein Seminary, Offices of Divine Worship in dioceses across our country, numerous Catholic Universities and Pastoral Institutes will offer workshops and publications to assist liturgical leaders in introducing and implementing the third typical edition of *The Roman Missal*. Since Rome granted the *recognitio* to the revised Order of Mass on June 23, 2008, music publishers have had almost two years to work on revising current Mass settings to fit the new wording of the third typical edition of *The Roman Missal*. In addition, they have commissioned a large number of new Mass settings, which will be published at the beginning of 2011. And so, the local leadership at the level of parishes, institutions, and religious communities will have more than ample help in preparing their people to pray using the liturgical texts in the third typical edition of *The Roman Missal*.

I am very grateful to the authors who have contributed to this book of essays:

- Reverend Andrew R. Wadsworth, MA, MA, GTCL, LTCL, LRAM, Executive Director of ICEL
- Monsignor Anthony Sherman, STD, Executive Director of the BCDW
- Monsignor James P. Moroney, STB, STL, past Executive Director of the BCDW
- Reverend Ronald Kunkel, STB, STL, STD (candidate), Professor of Liturgy at University of St. Mary of the Lake / Mundelein Seminary
- Reverend Paul Turner, STD, Pastor, Author, and Liturgical Consultant
- Reverend James Presta, STD, Mariologist and Professor at University of St. Mary of the Lake / Mundelein Seminary
- Jerry Galipeau, DMIN, Associate Publisher at World Library Publications
- Reverend Ronald Lewinski, STL, Pastor and past Director of the Chicago Office for Divine Worship
- Reverend Robert Tuzik, STL, PHD, former Professor of Liturgy at University of St. Mary of the Lake / Mundelein Seminary and currently consultant to myself, USCCB, Vox Clara, and our Chicago Office for Divine Worship.

I hope you find the contributions of these authors will assist you in exploring the many improvements that you will find in the third typical edition of *The Roman Missal*. I invite you to join me in praying for the successful implementation of the third typical edition of *The Roman Missal*, which will begin to be used in all the dioceses and religious institutions in the United States on the First Sunday of Advent, November 27, 2011.

Sincerely yours in Christ,

Francis Cardinal George, OMI
Archbishop of Chicago

Chapter 1

The Role of the International Commission on English in the Liturgy in Producing the Third Typical Edition of *The Roman Missal*

Monsignor Andrew R. Wadsworth, MA, MA, GTCL, LTCL, LRAM

I am delighted to have this opportunity to give an account of the role of the International Commission on English in the Liturgy (ICEL) in producing a translation of the third typical edition of the *Missale Romanum*, the Latin text of which was issued by the Holy See in 2002 and amended in 2008. As you may know, ICEL is a commission of eleven bishops representing the eleven largest territories where English is spoken. Since 1963 it has produced liturgical texts in English, translating the Missal, The Liturgy of the Hours, and all the sacramental rites. ICEL's work is coordinated by a secretariat which has been based in Washington, D.C., since its inception.

In considering ICEL's role, I would like to set my account in the broader context of the evolution of the English translation of the Missal and the use of the vernacular in Catholic liturgy. Any discussion of Catholic liturgy in English is inevitably linked to the Second Vatican Council. In the first decree to be issued from the Council, the Fathers wrote:

In order that the Christian people may more surely derive an abundance of graces from the liturgy, the Church desires to undertake with great care a general reform of the liturgy itself.[1]

The statement of this intention essentially implied two distinct processes which would consequently result in a liturgical revolution for Catholics of the Roman Rite: a radical revision of the liturgy of the Roman Rite resulting in new liturgical books which were not merely redactions of their predecessors but included ancient liturgical texts together with texts of more recent composition and subsequently the translation of these texts into vernacular languages.

It is important to consider these two issues together, as from the time of the Council they are virtually inseparable in the experience of the majority of Catholics. More than 40 years later, if asked what liturgical changes resulted from the Council, many Catholics would simply state that in the celebration of Mass the priest began to face the people and that Mass was said in English rather than in Latin. It comes as a shock to many people to realize that both of these developments have a much longer history and that neither of them was explicitly mandated by the Council or its decrees, although some, perhaps most, would argue that they are implicit in its formulations.

The idea of liturgy in the vernacular is as old as the Church herself, just as the parallel notion of a hieratic or sacred language used in worship is considerably more ancient than Christianity. The complex relationship between the use of both Latin and Greek, in the little we know of the earliest forms of Catholic liturgy, bears witness to the juxtaposition of these two ideas in the development of that liturgy through the centuries.

Toward the end of the first millennium, the missionary experience of the Church in the East led reformers such as Saints Cyril and Methodius to advocate the liturgical use of vernacular languages as a means of deepening comprehension of the celebration of the sacred mysteries. The Council of Trent considered the issue of vernacular celebration[2] in its sessions, largely although not exclusively in response to the Protestant Reformation. Its resistance of the notion

---

1. *Sacrosanctum Concilium*, 21

2. In its twenty-second Session, September 17, 1562. In the eighth chapter, the Council decreed, "Although the Mass contains much instruction for the faithful, it has, nevertheless, not been deemed advisable by the fathers that it should be celebrated everywhere [*passim*] in

at that stage led to the clarification and codification of Latin as the sole liturgical language of the Roman Rite.

In many places the use of the vernacular in liturgical song and devotional prayers for private (and sometimes public) recitation during the liturgy ensured that the idea of a vernacular element in liturgy was kept alive in the experience of many Catholics. This was particularly true in Germany where metrical settings of German texts of the Ordinary of the Mass were frequently sung from the seventeenth century onwards. In an increasing number of countries where English was spoken, English hymnody and devotions were also greatly in evidence. Out of this popular culture, there grew a movement for increased use of the vernacular, a movement that gathered momentum in the years immediately preceding the Second Vatican Council.[3]

In the fall of 1962, with the Second Vatican Council still in session, several English-speaking bishops met in Rome to discuss the production of the vernacular translations that they anticipated would be authorized by the Council. These bishops envisaged forming a committee which would produce uniform translations for all English-speaking countries. Their deliberations led to the formation of the International Committee (later, Commission) on English in the Liturgy. The first formal meeting of ICEL took place on October 17, 1963, and included representatives of the following English-speaking national Conferences of Bishops: Australia, Canada, England and Wales, India, Ireland, New Zealand, Pakistan, Scotland, South Africa, and the United States of America. In 1967, The Philippines would become the eleventh member of the Conference.

In October 1964, these same bishops drew up a formal mandate defining the nature and scope of the work of the Commission, which was to involve the translation of the Latin liturgical texts and the provision of original texts for the liturgy where required, and affirming the role of the Conferences in designating their Bishop representative on the Commission and in accepting or rejecting the final results of the work. This mandate was promptly approved by the Conferences. The bishops designated to represent their respective

---

the vernacular tongue. Also, if anyone says, 'The Mass ought to be celebrated in the vernacular tongue only' (*lingua tantum vulgari*), let him be anathema."

3. For an extensive account of this process, see Keith F. Pecklers, SJ, *Dynamic Equivalence*: *The Living Language of Christian Worship* (Collegeville, Minnesota: The Liturgical Press, 2003).

Conference of Bishops constituted ICEL's Episcopal Board. From the beginning the Board had the responsibility for governing ICEL, approving all projects undertaken by ICEL on behalf of the Conferences of Bishops, determining when a text is final, definitive, and ready for submission to the Conferences for their canonical vote, and approving the finances and the allocation of funds to carry out the work. Assisting the bishops was a second body called the Advisory Committee, which was composed of liturgical experts appointed by the Episcopal Board to oversee and carry out the work. As it was the primary body engaged in the work, the members of the Advisory Committee had great influence in determining the style of translation and the gradual evolution of that style and the approach to translation over the first thirty years of ICEL's history. The work itself was to be coordinated by a small team based at the ICEL Secretariat in Washington, D.C. During its first few years, ICEL's efforts were primarily devoted to the development of procedures and principles of translation.

In 1967, ICEL produced its first official English translation of a liturgical text, the Roman Canon (Eucharistic Prayer I). The translation provoked considerable controversy and opinion was clearly divided. *Worship*, the influential journal published by Saint John's Abbey, Collegeville, Minnesota, had long advocated use of the vernacular in the liturgy. In fact it had changed its name from *Orate Fratres* in 1951 precisely because it was thought inappropriate for a journal promoting the vernacular to have a Latin title. Godfrey Diekmann, OSB, a monk of Saint John's Abbey, was editor of the journal at the time of this title change. In 1967, Godfrey Diekmann was still editor of *Worship* and was by then also a member of the ICEL Advisory Committee responsible for its translation of the Roman Canon. Frederick McManus, one of the associate editors, later wrote:

> It was a very professional project, featuring the collaboration as consultants of a hundred or more experts in liturgy, Scripture, Christian Latin, English style, speech, and related fields. Perhaps only those with some personal experience of the problems involved in translating the Roman Canon can fully appreciate the achievement . . . we think this text compares very favorably not only with all existing English translations of the

Canon but also with current translations into other modern European languages. We are fortunate to have it.[4]

This quotation is from an article by Aelred Tegels, OSB, whose "Chronicle" column in *Worship* described developments in the liturgy as the instructions of the Council were implemented. An account of the history of ICEL by its then executive secretary, Doctor John Page,[5] mentions that the provisional ICEL translation of the Roman Canon issued in 1967 was "generally applauded"[6] though he acknowledged that there were some critics.

It is now widely accepted that much that is ascribed to the Second Vatican Council was in fact the work of the Consilium for the Implementation of the *Constitution on the Sacred Liturgy* (hereafter, Consilium), a curial committee charged with the task of implementing the provisions of *Sacrosanctum Concilium* by making concrete proposals. The Consilium rapidly identified the use of the vernacular as a key to increased participation on the part of the laity, hence the emphasis on vernacular translation and the speed with which the English translation was prepared. The Consilium eventually outlined its guidelines for the translation of liturgical texts in its Instruction, *Comme le prévoit* (January 25, 1969). In setting out the process, the Instruction states that:

> It is the duty of the episcopal conferences to decide which texts are to be translated, to prepare or review the translations, to approve them, and "after approval, that is, confirmation, by the Holy See" to promulgate them . . . .[7]

In order to facilitate this process, it goes on to suggest that

> When a common language is spoken in several different countries, international commissions should be appointed by the conferences of bishops who speak the same language to make one text for all.[8]

---

4. Aelred Tegels, "Chronicle," *Worship*, November, 1967, page 562.

5. John R. Page, PHD, Associate Editor of ICEL 1972–1974; Associate Secretary 1974–1980; Executive Secretary 1980–2002.

6. John R. Page, "ICEL, 1966–1989: Weaving the Words of our Common Christian Prayer," in *Shaping English Liturgy*, edited by Peter C. Finn and James M. Schellman (Washington, D.C.: The Pastoral Press, 1990), page 474.

7. *Comme le prévoit*, 2.

8. Ibid., quoting a letter of Cardinal Lercaro to the presidents of episcopal conferences, dated October 16, 1964.

There follows a careful statement of the parameters of the process whereby translations are produced, evaluated and approved. This includes a summary of the principles which govern the actual work of translation:

> The purpose of liturgical translations is to proclaim the message of salvation to believers and to express the prayer of the Church to the Lord: "Liturgical translations have become . . . the voice of the Church" (address of Paul VI to participants in the congress on translations of liturgical texts, 10 November 1965). To achieve this end, it is not sufficient that a liturgical translation merely reproduce the expressions and ideas of the original text. Rather it must faithfully communicate to a given people, and in their own language, that which the Church by means of this given text originally intended to communicate to another people in another time. A faithful translation, therefore, cannot be judged on the basis of individual words: the total context of this specific act of communication must be kept in mind, as well as the literary form proper to the respective language.[9]

The Instruction goes on to underline the necessity of taking great care in the translation of Latin terms and idioms that are difficult to render in vernacular languages or present obstacles in a contemporary context not foreseen in the original text. The central maxim of *Comme le prévoit* expresses it thus:

> The accuracy and value of a translation can only be assessed in terms of the purpose of the communication.[10]

From technical details of translation theory, the Instruction passes to rather more logistical considerations suggesting that:

> Those countries which have a common language should employ a "mixed commission" to prepare a single text. There are many advantages to such a procedure: in the preparation of a text the most competent experts are able to cooperate; a unique possibility for communication is created among these people; participation of the people is made easier. In this joint venture between countries speaking the same language it is important to distinguish between the texts which are said by one person and heard by the congregation and those intended to be recited or sung by all. Uniformity is obviously more important for the latter category than for the former.

---

9. Ibid., 6.
10. Ibid., 14.

In those cases where a single text is prepared for a large number of countries, the text should satisfy the "different needs and mentalities of each region. . . .[11]

By the time *Comme le prévoit* was published, the process of translation was already underway, often guided by scholars whose opinions became authoritative, such as Father Antoine Dumas, OSB, a member of the Consilium, who wrote extensively about the semantic content of the vocabulary of the Missal. More recent scholarship would suggest that some of his dogmatic views regarding translation are held to be less authoritative now than at the time when he published them, although opinion remains divided.[12]

It is reasonable to conclude that the Instruction *Comme le prévoit* became the charter not only for ICEL's translation work but also for the production of original texts. These original texts are prayers composed in a vernacular language (in this case, English) and not based on any Latin original. They are then inserted into the translation of the Latin text as a supplementary element. The 1973 translation of *The Roman Missal* contains a number of original compositions called "Alternative Opening Prayers." Such texts are mentioned in *Comme le prévoit*:

> Texts translated from another language are clearly not sufficient for the celebration of a fully renewed liturgy. The creation of new texts will be necessary. But translation of texts transmitted through the tradition of the Church is the best school and discipline for the creation of new texts so "that any new forms adopted should in some way grow organically from forms already in existence."[13]

Comme le prévoit was issued after the Consilium had considered the recommendations of a special study group on translation. According to Monsignor Frederick McManus, a founding member of ICEL, *Comme le prévoit* greatly benefited from the experience of ICEL,

---

11. Ibid., 41–42; once again quoting the letter of Cardinal Lercaro of October 16, 1964.

12. Antoine Dumas, OSB, "Pour Mieux Comprendre Les Textes Liturgiques Du Missel Romain" in *Notitiae* 6, 1970. For different appreciations of the contribution of Dumas, see Lauren Pristas, "The Collects at Sunday Mass: An examination of the Revisions of Vatican II" in *Nova et Vetera*, 3:1 (Winter, 2005): 5-38 and "Appreciating the Collect—An Irenic Methodology" edited by James G. Leachman, OSB, and Daniel P. McCarthy, OSB (Farnborough Hampshire, England: St. Michael's Abbey Press, 2008).

13. Ibid, 43, quoting *Sacrosanctum Concilium*, 23.

whose (future) executive secretary[14] served on a study group of the Consilium for this purpose.

The formation of this study group, according to Archbishop Annibale Bugnini, then Secretary of the Consilium (and later Secretary of the Congregation for Divine Worship), was proposed at a meeting of the Presidential Council of the Consilium in April 1967. He referred to the purpose of the new study group as "the translation of liturgical texts into the vernaculars." According to Archbishop Bugnini, the Instruction was reviewed and corrected by Pope Paul VI from an Italian version of the text. In a letter sent to Pope Paul VI along with the document, Bugnini writes:

> It was said that the norms were not binding in the same degree as a liturgical book; they were rather a working tool that brought together in a systematic form the general and particular regulations issued by the *Consilium* during the previous five years.[15]

The text of the Instruction was published in the journal of the Congregation for Divine Worship, *Notitiae*, but it never appeared in the official *Acta Apostolicae Sedis,* the official record of the Holy See. ICEL was asked by the Consilium to prepare an English text of *Comme le prévoit* from the original (French, with some additions in Italian), which would then be sent to the Conferences of Bishops.

Though *Comme le prévoit* appears to contain the first mention in a Vatican document of the possibility of original texts being added alongside the translations of Latin texts, five years earlier, the mandate for ICEL had already listed among its functions: "To work out a plan for the translation of liturgical texts and the *provision of original texts* where required."[16] Furthermore, according to McManus:

---

14. Monsignor McManus was a member of the ICEL advisory committee since its foundation in 1963. He was also Executive Director of the United States Bishops' Committee on the Liturgy and President of the Liturgical Conference. He was a peritus at Vatican II serving on the preparatory liturgical commission and the Consilium.

15. Archbishop Annibale Bugnini, *The Reform of the Liturgy 1948–1975* (Collegeville, Minnesota: The Liturgical Press, 1990). Translated by Matthew J. O'Connell, page 238.

16. The mandate was printed in a booklet issued by ICEL called *English in the Liturgy.* It has been reprinted in Jeffrey Michael Kemper, *Behind the Text: A Study of the Principles and Procedures of Translation, Adaptation, and Composition of Original Texts by the International Commission on English in the Liturgy*, PʜD Thesis, University of Notre Dame, 1993, Appendix 1, page 366.

Later it became even more evident that, while the primary task was the translation of Latin texts, liturgical development and adaptation would ultimately demand much more by way of creativity. At the end of the 1960s, this became one of the normative principles of the liturgical books themselves: they regularly left to the conference of bishops—and thus to their instrumentalities, the joint or international commissions like ICEL—the creation of new vernacular liturgical prayers wherever the Roman books offered alternatives.[17]

In a 1990 article on ICEL's original texts, Sister Kathleen Hughes, RSCJ, a member of the ICEL Advisory Committee and of its Subcommittee on Original Texts for many years, states that the 1973 English translation of *The Roman Missal* "was the only vernacular translation of the *Missale Romanum* to incorporate original compositions in a first edition."[18] In fact when *Comme le prévoit* was published in 1969, "ICEL's Advisory Committee expanded its work on the collects to incorporate the composition of alternative prayers."[19]

It is important to note at this stage that there is no evidence here that the Bishops' Conferences, or even the individual Bishop-representatives on the Episcopal Board, were consulted before this decision was made. Furthermore, there seems to have been no spontaneous request from any Bishops' Conference for the composition of original prayers. Although it has been stated that these original compositions were based on the Latin prayers, they "represented considerable original elaboration and development of the Latin."[20] These were presented to the bishops as "alternative prayers" with a note which said the new texts "remained within the norms of legitimate liturgical translation." A justification from *Comme le prévoit* was cited, not article 43 on original texts as might be expected, but article 34, which justifies a free translation from the Latin by using amplification and paraphrase. The Foreword by the USCCB to *The Sacramentary* [1974] states:

---

17. McManus, "ICEL: The First Years" in *Shaping English Liturgy*, page 448.

18. Sister H. Kathleen Hughes, RSCJ, "Original Texts: Beginnings, Present Projects, Guidelines" in *Shaping English Liturgy*, page 219.

19. Ibid., page 221.

20. Ibid., page 223.

The alternative opening prayers are not direct or faithful translations of the corresponding Latin text. They follow its theme or are inspired by it, but they are generally more concrete and expansive.[21]

The Foreword adds that these prayers were "prompted" by article 43 of *Comme le prévoit*. That is, by the paragraph that speaks of the "creation of new texts," not by the paragraph on amplification that was cited in the original consultation to justify these same texts.

ICEL's work on original texts continued after the first translation of the Missal was completed. Its long-term project to revise the translations of all the liturgical books included plans for more original prayers.[22] In 1982, ICEL set up its Subcommittee on Original Texts to concentrate on this work, until then part of the work of a Subcommittee on Translations, Revisions and Original Texts. Sister Kathleen Hughes was appointed the first chairman of this new subcommittee.

At the time of the production of the 1973 edition of the Missal, it was envisaged that a revision of the translation would in time be both necessary and desirable. In order to facilitate the implementation of the liturgical renewal desired by the Council Fathers, the Holy See published five documents of special importance, each successively numbered as an "Instruction for the Right Application of the Constitution on the Sacred Liturgy of the Second Vatican Council."

The first of these Instructions, *Inter oecumenici*, was issued by the Sacred Congregation of Rites and the Consilium on September 26, 1964, and contained initial general principles for the orderly carrying out of the liturgical renewal. Three years later, on May 4, 1967, a second Instruction was issued, *Tres abhinc annos*. This described further adaptations to the Order of Mass. The third Instruction, *Liturgicae instaurationes*, of September 5, 1970, was issued by the Sacred Congregation for Divine Worship, the body that succeeded the Sacred Congregation of Rites and the Consilium. It provided directives on the central role of the Bishop in the renewal of the liturgy throughout a diocese.

With Pope John Paul II's Apostolic Letter *Vicesimus quintus annus*, issued on 4 December 1988 to mark the 25th anniversary of

---

21. "Foreword to the Sacramentary," *The Sacramentary* (Collegeville, Minnesota: The Liturgical Press, 1974), page 14.

22. A detailed account of ICEL's principles and procedures for revision of rites is given by Jeffrey Michael Kemper; see note 15.

Sacrosanctum Concilium, there began a gradual process of evaluation, completion, and consolidation of the liturgical renewal.[23] On January 25, 1994, the Congregation for Divine Worship and the Discipline of the Sacraments carried this process forward by issuing the Fourth Instruction, *Varietates legitimae*, concerning difficult questions on the Roman Liturgy and inculturation or adaptations for local churches.

In February of 1997, Pope John Paul II asked the Congregation for Divine Worship and the Discipline of the Sacraments to carry forward the process of the liturgical renewal by codifying the conclusions of its work in collaboration with the bishops over the years regarding the question of the liturgical translations. ICEL had done much, particularly during the eighties and nineties, in order to establish what would be expected in a revision of the earlier English translation. Several ideas emerged as a result of this survey—it was felt that liturgical language should generally be more formal, reflecting to a greater degree the richness of the original texts and it was also widely held that mistakes in the current translation should be corrected.

A draft revision of the Missal was prepared by ICEL and submitted to the Congregation in 1997 after a long and scholarly process of preparation. The translation was prepared in accordance with the provisions of *Comme le prévoit* but with a stricter approach to the demands of fidelity to the meaning of the original Latin text. During this same period, the Holy See was carefully considering a fuller statement of the principles that should govern the production of vernacular translations. This process of reflection resulted in the suspension of the approval of the draft Missal text approved by the eleven ICEL member Bishops' Conferences in June 1997 while the clarification of the principles of translation was in progress.

In a letter to Bishop Maurice Taylor, then chairman of ICEL, on October 26, 1999, Cardinal Jorge Medina Estévez of the Congregation for Divine Worship stressed that the activities of the Mixed Commission (ICEL) were to be defined as the translation into English of the *editiones typicae* of the Roman liturgical texts and books in their integrity. Consequently, any proposals for cultural adaptation, modification, or the composition of original texts were to remain the

---

23. The most authoritative account of the ICEL story, 1963–1990, is to be found in *Shaping the English Liturgy*, edited by Peter C. Finn and James M. Schellman (Washington, D.C.: The Pastoral Press, 1990).

province of the individual Bishops' Conferences, according to the norms of the 1994 Instruction, *Varietates legitimae*, and the texts were to remain subject to the approval of the Holy See.

Cardinal Francis George, the United States representative to the Episcopal Board of ICEL, explained to the United States Bishops' Conference that the point of the Holy See's clarification was that ICEL was not to generate original texts; but rather, that requests for such texts must come from a Conference of Bishops.

The Congregation for Divine Worship published its clarification of the principles of translation in the Fifth Instruction "For the Right Implementation of the Constitution on the Sacred Liturgy of the Second Vatican Council," *Liturgiam authenticam: On the Use of Vernacular Languages in the Publication of the Books of the Roman Liturgy.* It was approved by Pope John Paul II on March, 28, 2001, and came in to force on April 25 of the same year. The press release issued by the Holy See gives a clear indication of the significance of this Instruction:

> The Fifth Instruction begins by referring to the initiative of the Council and the work of the successive Popes and the Bishops throughout the world, recalling the successes of the liturgical reform, while at the same time noting the continued vigilance needed in order to preserve the identity and unity of the Roman Rite throughout the world. In this regard, the Instruction takes up the observations made in 1988 by Pope John Paul II calling for progress beyond an initial phase to one of improved translations of liturgical texts. Accordingly, *Liturgiam authenticam* offers the Latin Church a new formulation of principles of translation with the benefit of more than thirty years' experience in the use of the vernacular in liturgical celebrations.

> *Liturgiam authenticam* supersedes all norms previously set forth on liturgical translation, with the exception of those in the Fourth Instruction *Varietates legitimae*, and specifies that the two Instructions should be read in conjunction with each other. It calls more than once for a new era in translation of liturgical texts.

> It should be noted that the new document substitutes for all previous norms while integrating much of their content, drawing them together in a more unified and systematic way, underpinning them with some careful reflection, and linking them to certain related questions that so far have been treated separately. Moreover, it is faced with the task of speaking in a few pages of principles applicable to several hundred languages currently

used in liturgical celebration in every part of the world. It does not employ the technical terminology of linguistics or of the human sciences but refers principally to the domain of pastoral experience.

Much can be said in relation to *Liturgiam authenticam* and much has already been published by way of commentary and evaluation of the effect of this important Instruction. My own concern here is to briefly assess its significance for ICEL and the task with which it is entrusted. The most far-reaching consequence is that the Instruction embodies an entirely different approach to translation. In order to illustrate this, we must consider several important aspects of translation theory which are pertinent in this regard.

Dynamic equivalence and *formal equivalence* are two quite different approaches to translation. Dynamic equivalence (also known as *functional equivalence*) attempts to convey the thought expressed in a source text (if necessary, at the expense of literalness, original word order, the source text's grammatical voice, etc.), while formal equivalence attempts to render the text word-for-word (if necessary, sometimes at the expense of what might be considered a more natural expression in the target language). The two approaches represent an emphasis, respectively, on readability and on literal fidelity to the source text. There is, however, in reality, no sharp boundary between dynamic and formal equivalence and elements of both approaches will often be evident in most translations. Broadly speaking, the two represent a spectrum of translation approaches, each approach having its own integrity and resulting in a translation that demonstrates characteristics in marked contrast to each other stylistically.

The terms *dynamic equivalence* and *formal equivalence* are associated with the translator Eugene Nida (born 1911), and were originally coined to describe ways of translating the scriptures, but the two approaches are applicable to any translation.

As dynamic equivalence does not require strict adherence to the grammatical structure of the original text in favor of a more natural rendering in the target language, it is most suited to texts where the readability of the translation is more important than the preservation of the original grammatical structure. Thus, a novel might be translated with greater use of dynamic equivalence so that it may read well, while in diplomacy or in some business settings there may be an insistence on formal equivalence because it is believed that fidelity to the grammatical structure of the language results in greater accuracy of translation.

The more the source language differs from the target language, the more challenges it may present in the production of a literal translation. On the other hand, formal equivalence can often allow readers or hearers to see how meaning was expressed in the original text, preserving idioms, rhetorical devices, and certain modes of speech. In case it is not already obvious, *Comme le prévoit* engendered the approach identified as dynamic equivalence whereas in *Liturgiam authenticam* there is a shift to formal equivalence.

Although both approaches as applied to liturgical translation have their advocates, opponents to *Liturgiam authenticam* in general and to the new translation of *The Roman Missal* in particular tend to be rather disingenuous, as their clearest motivation would seem to be to scupper the use of formal equivalence for reasons of an ecclesiological rather than a liturgical or linguistic nature. An example of this would be the view that texts should only "arise" out of the local church, which should be the sole source of their approbation. This sort of congregationalism militates against any sense of a common identity for the Roman Rite. Given the legitimate diversity of style in liturgical celebration permitted by the norms, a sense of the unity of the Roman Rite remains essentially a textual unity—we all use the same liturgical texts when we celebrate the liturgy. Frequently critics reach across the experience of the last 40 years and claim a principle in *Sacrosanctum Concilium* that ignores the Church's established process of putting that same principle into practice.[24] There can also be a tendency to ignore the fact that at the time *Sacrosanctum Concilium* was written everyone in the Latin Rite was still using what we now call the Extraordinary Form and that the new Missal text (*Missale Romanum* 1969), including both ancient texts and those of more recent composition, was yet to be assembled.

The difference in approaches to translation is most clearly demonstrated by comparison. Here we have the Collect of the Mass of Christmas Day, a text from the seventh century *Veronese Sacramentary:*[25]

---

24. *Sacrosanctum Concilium*, 40, is often cited in this way in relation to inculturation and experimentation in the liturgy.

25. *Sacramentarium Veronese* (Rome: Herder, Editrice Libreria, 1978, 1239), page 157.

Missale Romanum [2002]	The Roman Missal [1973]	The Roman Missal [2010]
Deus, qui humánae substántiae dignitátem	Lord God, we praise you for creating man,	O God, who wonderfully created the dignity of human nature
et mirabíliter condidisti, et mirabílius reformásti,	and still more for restoring him in Christ.	and still more wonderfully restored it,
da, quaésumus, nobis eius divinitátis esse consórtes,	Your Son shared our weakness; may we share his glory, . . .	grant, we pray, that we may share in the divinity of Christ,
qui humanitátis nostrae fíeri dignátus est párticeps.		who humbled himself to share in our humanity.

On a practical level, the consequences of *Liturgiam authenticam* for ICEL have been profound. Not only was it necessary to abandon an approach to translation that had characterized the earlier edition of the Missal, it was also necessary to take on a new management structure expressive of a new relationship with Episcopal Conferences and the Holy See. This resulted in new statutes for ICEL, now formally recognized as a "mixed commission" by the Congregation for Divine Worship. In July 2001, Bishop Arthur Roche of Leeds succeeded Bishop Maurice Taylor as Chairman. In September of that same year, Monsignor Bruce Harbert[26] succeeded Doctor John Page as General Secretary of the Commission and Executive Director of its Secretariat.

These changes were immediately followed by the publication of the third typical edition of the *Missale Romanum* on May 2, 2002, the new Latin edition of *The Roman Missal* which would be the first text ICEL would have to translate in accordance with the new directives. For a complex variety of reasons, it was not felt possible that a revision of the 1997 translation would be possible, so an entirely new translation was begun. Consequently it is not strictly accurate to speak of the translation as a revision, as it is a new translation of the most recent Latin text of the Missal.

This new edition of the Missal contains a revised and expanded version of the *General Instruction of the Roman Missal* (increased from 357 to 399 paragraphs). The corpus of texts for the Prayers over the People has been expanded, allowing for a different text of this prayer

---

26. 2002–2009.

to be assigned to each day of Lent. The third edition also provided liturgical texts for the celebration of 22 saints and various other memorials that have been added to the General Roman Calendar since 1975. The Missal has introduced new Mass formularies for the Common of the Blessed Virgin Mary, for Masses for Various Needs and Occasions, and for Votive Masses. The Appendix to the Order of Mass now provides the texts of the Eucharistic Prayers for Reconciliation and the Eucharistic Prayer for Masses for Various Needs and Intentions. In addition to the provision of additional texts, the third edition also contains a greatly expanded corpus of chants, including the complete settings of Eucharistic Prayers I–IV. The reprint of this Missal in 2008 contained further changes and additions to liturgical texts which now include Vigil Masses for the solemnities of the Epiphany and the Ascension of the Lord and for the celebration of the Vigil Mass of Pentecost in the extended form (in the manner of the Easter Vigil) with additional readings and with a prayer following each reading.

The principles by which the translation of *The Roman Missal* has been prepared are enunciated in two texts issued by the Congregation for Divine Worship, *Liturgiam authenticam* (2001) and the *Ratio Translationis for the English Language* (2007) in which the principles are further explained and their application illustrated with examples. The principles that have guided the preparation of the new translation seek to render more faithfully and fully the content of the original Latin texts, with respect to the style, vocabulary, and register of the language used and with a care for the demands of the public proclamation and singing of the texts. In this last respect, ICEL has commissioned a small panel of highly skilled and experienced Church musicians to undertake the setting of the English texts to chant for inclusion in the Missal.

Obviously it is of great importance that those preparing and reviewing the draft translations have a necessary knowledge of Latin to ensure that the meaning of the original is faithfully conveyed. Although the formal process of preparing the new translation has taken eight years, the remote preparation for those most intimately involved in this work is more in terms of a lifetime, as the acquisition of the various skills required to a sufficiently high level takes many years. Furthermore, ICEL has the considerable advantage of over 45 years of experience in this field and as I write, three of our five staff at the Secretariat have jointly served ICEL for over a century. This means that there is already a living tradition at work in this process and that the organization has a human memory.

The process that each text goes through in the effort to establish an English text acceptable to the Episcopal Conferences and the Holy See is lengthy and complex. Each text is initially translated by a base translator who has received a *nihil obstat* from the Congregation for Divine Worship. The base translation is then evaluated by a team of reviewers whose comments serve to amend the text as necessary. The resulting text, with the comments of the experts, is provided to the Roman Missal Editorial Committee, a committee of four bishops assisted by various experts (ordained and lay, male and female, including religious) which reworks the text for submission to the Bishops of the Commission.

The Bishops of the Commission each study the translation before gathering as a group. During the meeting they read the texts aloud and discuss alternatives. When a translation of a section of the Missal is complete, the bishops vote to include the texts in a Green Book (or Study Book) that is distributed to the Conferences of Bishops—typically for a six-month review. The bishops of the member Conferences are free to seek the opinion of whomever they choose in preparing observations on the draft texts. The comments of the Conferences are then submitted to ICEL, where again the text is reviewed and altered in light of the comments. The resulting text is then voted on by the Bishops of the Commission for inclusion in the Gray Book, or text for the canonical vote of the Conferences.

Once a Bishops' Conference has approved a text, the Gray Book is sent by the member Conference to the Congregation for Divine Worship and the Discipline of the Sacraments with a request for its authorization. This request is called the *relatio*. A Conference may at this stage request specific adaptations or amendment of the text based on the pastoral demands of its territory. Since 2002, the Congregation for Divine Worship has been assisted in its task of assessing the English translation of *The Roman Missal* by a committee of Bishops and other suitably qualified scholars. This consultative committee of bishops and other experts is called *Vox Clara* and has met nineteen times in Rome under the chairmanship of Cardinal George Pell of Sydney.

In a letter to Cardinal Jorge Arturo Medina Estévez, then Prefect of the Congregation for Divine Worship and the Discipline of the Sacraments, Pope John Paul II explained that Vox Clara "has been established to assist and advise the Congregation for Divine Worship and the Discipline of the Sacraments in fulfilling its responsibilities with regard to the English translations of liturgical texts. Representing the different continents as it does, the committee reflects the international character of the English language. This makes available to the Holy See the great wealth of pastoral experience drawn from different cultures."[27]

The Holy See grants its authorization of a liturgical text in a *recognitio*, or decree of approval. At that point, the ICEL Secretariat assists member Conferences in preparing this definitive text in such a way that it may be sent to publishers for the publication of the Missal. It is for Bishops' Conferences in conjunction with the Holy See to determine when a liturgical text should be implemented in their territory.

The more complex a process becomes, the more unwieldy it is in its administration and the longer it takes. It would be entirely impractical and inappropriate to administer a process of consultation beyond that which has been outlined above. In such a case, the chances of achieving a translation of any quality would be seriously diminished, if not entirely removed. Some have suggested that the bishops have been passive victims in this process rather than its protagonists. This perpetuates the myth that the translation is the work of the few who in complete abstraction from the life of the Church have produced a text which they now seek to foist on everyone else.

Sadly, in some quarters, there has been a studied obfuscation on the part of critics of the proposed translation in relation to the actual process whereby it has been prepared. I hope the clarifications of this essay are of assistance in transmitting an accurate account of that process in its evolution. One of the principle emphases of *Liturgiam authenticam* is that bishops should actively undertake the responsibility to provide liturgical texts in the language(s) of their territory. For that reason, it is true to say that bishops are involved at every stage of the process and a number of the bishops are themselves translators. It is

---

27. A letter of Pope John Paul II to Cardinal Jorge Arturo Medina Estévez (April 20, 2002).

also important to state that ICEL is an agency that unambiguously supports the bishops in meeting their responsibility in this regard. The texts have been offered for consultation and comment at each stage of their preparation and the reactions of Episcopal Conferences have had a major influence on the evolution of the texts. The approval of the text by at least a two-thirds majority vote of each member Conference has been the determining factor in the progress of the translation. In this sense, the translation is a true work of the Church, a witness to the collaboration possible between the Church's pastors and all those who seek to serve the Church in enriching her liturgical life. It may also be useful to underline that the Holy See has always had the last say in the process of the authorization of texts for liturgical use and in the case of sacramental formulas. This responsibility is reserved to the Pope alone.

A frequent observation heard in relation to the new translation of *The Roman Missal* is that the language is of a more formal character than that of the current translation. This was an intention in the production of the translation and so is clearly identifiable as one of its characteristics. The aim was to reflect features of the original Latin texts, providing a translation which is clearly sacral in character and yet not archaic in style.

In order to appreciate this feature of the text, we need to rid ourselves of the idea that the sole purpose of language is communication of information. This idea has a tendency to inculcate minimalism in the use of language, as it would argue that clarity of communication is best achieved by using the fewest words possible. This tendency is immediately evident in two widely spoken languages, English and Spanish, as the demands of a world language have understandably led to a simplification of vocabulary and structures in an effort to ensure comprehensibility for the greatest number of those using these languages. The result is inevitably an impoverishment of the language, as the register[28] of everyday conversational language becomes the norm guiding not only spoken but also written forms of the language. These considerations of register and vocabulary are particularly important in relation to liturgical texts as we use vernacular translations of texts

---

28. In linguistics, a *register* is a variety of language used for a particular purpose or in a particular setting.

originally in Latin or sometimes Greek or Hebrew—languages which often seem far removed from our everyday use of English.

In later antiquity, as Latin developed into something of a world language, the breakdown of its syntax and morphology followed rapidly. The Latin of the majority of the orations of the liturgy, however, belongs to an earlier period when the purity of style and economy of expression were distinctive features. The vocabulary of these prayers is necessarily rich as it reflects the various mysteries of salvation, conveying concepts which do not always occur in everyday conversation. To simplify the language radically is often to dilute the concept, frequently omitting a distinctive feature communicated in the original. A procession of such simplifications often leads to a paraphrase of the original or a complete change in meaning from that which was originally intended.

Wherever liturgical vocabulary is unfamiliar in a pastoral context, there is a clear need to engage in catechesis. In this way, familiar concepts are broadened and unfamiliar ideas are explained so that the quality of our liturgical celebrations is enriched not only in its constituent elements but also in the depth of participation of those who engage in its celebration. For this reason, the Council's *Sacrosanctum Concilium* contains the following exhortation: "with zeal and patience, pastors of souls must promote the liturgical instruction of the faithful, and also their active participation in the liturgy both internally and externally."[29] Failure to do so does not diminish the need to carry out such catechesis. Many have lamented the lack of real catechesis that accompanied the implementation of the *Missale Romanum* of Paul VI [1969]. We have to hope that the implementation of the new translation will not be a missed opportunity in this regard.

Our liturgical language not only has the purpose of communicating the content of our belief, but it also needs to express that belief by giving voice to the mind of the Church in celebrating a particular mystery and the heart of those engaging in the liturgical celebration. In this, text is often wedded to liturgical song, which heightens its proclamation and shows a commonality of characteristics with poetry and song in other contexts. The single most readily identifiable source

---

29. *Sacrosanctum Concilium*, 19.

of our liturgical texts is sacred scripture, whose own textual features owe much to the devices of poetry and exigencies of song.

It has been a particular goal of the new translation that allusions to scripture will be more clearly evidenced. In this way, it is also rendered possible to make all liturgical catechesis a means of further deepening a spirituality which is rooted in the Church's reading of the scriptures.

The process of widespread catechesis that must prepare and accompany the implementation of the new translation of the Missal is an example of a primary work of the Church, teaching the faith and helping people to a richer, deeper experience of that faith, particularly in their celebration of the liturgy. Obviously the implementation of a new translation after 40 years of using the current text necessitates careful preparation. Most people have a natural reticence in relation to change of any sort and the reception of the Missal can be greatly assisted if the process by which it was prepared, the features of the text, a general catechesis on the nature of the liturgy in general and the celebration of the Eucharist in particular are undertaken on the widest possible scale. Priests will certainly need assistance and encouragement in adapting to the demands of a text which initially will be unfamiliar.

It is natural that this catechetical opportunity should not be missed. To this end, ICEL commissioned a multi-media catechetical resource entitled *Become One Body, One Spirit in Christ*. This interactive DVD contains much video footage of those who were most intimately involved in the production of the new translation and interviews from all over the English-speaking world, along with a vast quantity of text files that offer an in-depth exploration of the riches of the text and the process of creating the Missal across the centuries. It is hoped that this and other similar initiatives will help us all to explore the treasures of the Missal for many years to come.

Some commentators have called for the implementation of new translations *ad experimentum* as a means of evaluating their suitability for more widespread use. Strictly speaking, it is not correct to speak of "times of experimentation" in relation to the production of the translation of liturgical texts, for this has not been the experience of the 40 years since the Second Vatican Council. It is more useful to consider the vast process of collaboration and consultation that has already taken place, which is essential to the production of vernacular liturgical texts and is the necessary prelude to the final authorization of such texts for liturgical use.

I offer this description of the translation process in order to show the relationships between the various people and groups who are working together to provide the Church with an English translation to meet the needs of the diverse community that it serves. Among the translators, consulters, and collaborators in this complex process are men and women who are distinguished not only by their scholarship and understanding of the liturgy but also by their experience as pastors, catechists, parish musicians, and in other roles concerned with our liturgy in cathedrals, parishes, and religious communities.

The whole purpose of the production of the English edition of the Missal and the guiding purpose in all of ICEL's activity is that a dignified celebration of the liturgy in which due attention has been given to each of the constitutive elements will enable all the people of God to come to a greater knowledge and experience of the saving mystery that we celebrate. A good translation should enable the people of God to celebrate the sacred mysteries in such a way "that their minds are attuned to their voices, and that they cooperate with divine grace, lest they receive it in vain."[30]

---

30. *Sacrosanctum Concilium*, 11; cf. 2 Corinthians 6:1.

Chapter 2

The United States Bishops' Committee on Divine Worship and the Reception of the New Translation of *The Roman Missal*

Monsignor Anthony F. Sherman, STD

THE ROLE OF THE USCCB COMMITTEE ON DIVINE WORSHIP

The Committee on Divine Worship is part of the United States Conference of Catholic Bishops (USCCB). The USCCB is an assembly of the hierarchy of the United States of America and the Virgin Islands who exercises certain pastoral functions on behalf of the Christian faithful of the United States. This body must address a host of different issues and it deals with many of them through seventeen committees, each with a Bishop chairman. Some of the committees have subcommittees; this is the case with the Committee on Divine Worship, which has a Subcommittee on Hispanics and the Liturgy.

The Committee, consisting of nine Bishop members, a Bishop consultant, and six non-Bishop consultants, is presently chaired by the Most Reverend Gregory M. Aymond. The Committee is assisted by the Secretariat of Divine Worship located in Washington, D.C. The Secretariat carries out the work of the Committee on Divine Worship, by:

- overseeing the preparation and approval of liturgical books and texts and granting the *concordat cum originali* for ritual publications of liturgical texts in the United States;
- reviewing all publications in the United States of America which contain excerpts from approved liturgical books;
- providing leadership in liturgical formation and sacramental catechesis, especially by means of its monthly *Newsletter* and other publications; and
- serving as a resource for bishops, diocesan liturgical commissions, and offices of worship seeking advice.

The mandate of the Committee is to assist the bishops of the Latin Church, both collectively and individually, in fulfilling their roles as shepherds responsible for the liturgical life of their communities. One of the mission responsibilities of the Committee is the translation of liturgical texts and the development of guidelines for the celebration of the Mass and the Sacraments. Most of the time, the Committee is engaged in enabling the bishops to review texts that have already been translated by the International Commission on English in the Liturgy (ICEL). The Committee becomes more directly involved in texts that are prepared for the Proper Calendar of the United States of America. In addition to these activities, the Committee also reviews liturgical participation aids and musical settings; responds to specific questions from bishops and provides information when requested to bishops and diocesan offices; and collaborates with USCCB Communications in the publications of liturgical text and rituals.

The Committee on Divine Worship has many external relationships that are critical for its work. Not only does it relate to the other committees that exist within the USCCB, but it maintains contact with dioceses and other liturgical groups. The Secretariat is available for liturgy directors and heads of offices who may have some specific liturgical questions or need clarification about some of the guidelines or directives issued either by the Committee or the Congregation for Divine Worship and the Discipline of the Sacraments (CDWDS).

An extremely important relationship is with the Holy See, especially with the CDWDS. When issues have been discussed and formulated by the Committee or the full body of bishops, the President of the USCCB will then contact the Congregation.

The art of translation requires experts who have had years of background and experience in Latin and Greek and are familiar with the way in which the use of words has evolved over the years. ICEL is the organization that coordinates these experts. It is this group that develops liturgical translations and then presents them to the Conferences for their evaluation. The Committee then has the responsibility to coordinate these reviews.

THE INTERNATIONAL COMMISSION ON ENGLISH IN THE LITURGY

ICEL is a mixed commission of Catholic Bishops' Conferences in countries where English is used in the celebration of the Liturgy according to the Roman rite. The Commission was founded in Rome in 1963 by the English-speaking countries at the Second Vatican Council. On September 15, 2003, the CDWDS formally established ICEL as a Mixed Commission.

The fundamental purpose of the Commission is to prepare English translations of the Latin liturgical books and any other liturgical texts. The rules and procedures to be followed by ICEL are very specifically laid down by two documents. The first document is the Fifth Instruction "For the Right Implementation of the Constitution on the Sacred Liturgy of the Second Vatican Council," *Liturgiam authenticam: On the Use of Vernacular Languages in the Publication of the Books of the Roman Liturgy* (LA), which was issued by the CDWDS on March 28, 2001. The second document is the *Ratio Translationis for the English Language*. The CDWDS published this document in 2007. These two documents not only govern the work of ICEL, but anyone who is involved in the various stages of liturgical translation needs to be familiar with them. Thus all of the bishops had to be aware of the context established by these documents, and when they consulted with others it was necessary that those advisors be aware of and remain within the parameters of those documents.

ICEL presently consists of eleven Conferences of Bishops: Australia, Canada, England and Wales, India, Ireland, New Zealand, Pakistan, the Philippines, Scotland, South Africa, and the United States of America. Each conference elects one Bishop to represent it at

ICEL. Other Conferences of Bishops in whose countries English is used in the liturgy may, on request, be admitted to associate participation in ICEL. The associate member conferences are: the Antilles, Bangladesh, CEPAC (Pacific Islands), Gambia-Liberia-Sierra Leone, Ghana, Kenya, Malaysia-Singapore, Malawi, Nigeria, Papua New Guinea and the Solomon Islands, Sri Lanka, Tanzania, Uganda, Zambia, and Zimbabwe. It is clear from the list of members that many different perspectives are brought to the table, and no one country has a monopoly on the outcome of any given final translation.

The work of the ICEL bishops is assisted by a professional staff located in Washington, D.C. The ICEL Secretariat coordinates the work of the specialists throughout the English-speaking world in the preparation of the translations.

The Translation Process and the Role of the Committee on Divine Worship

In developing any liturgical translation, the first step in the ICEL process is the development of what is known as a base text. The translators, at this point, make sure that all of the words in the particular Latin prayer are accounted for, as well as the particular Latin syntax. This translation is an extremely unrefined one and must then be worked on by other translators in an effort to develop a text that will be able to meet the criteria determined in LA.

The rules provided for the translators are quite detailed in scope:

> The Latin liturgical texts of the Roman Rite, while drawing on centuries of ecclesial experience in transmitting the faith of the Church received from the Fathers, are themselves the fruit of the liturgical renewal, just recently brought forth. In order that such a rich patrimony may be preserved and passed on through the centuries, it is to be kept in mind from the beginning that the translation of the liturgical texts of the Roman Liturgy is not so much a work of creative innovation as it is of rendering the original texts faithfully and accurately into the vernacular language. While it is permissible to arrange the wording, the syntax and the style in such a way as to prepare a flowing vernacular text suitable to the rhythm of popular prayer, the original text, insofar as possible, must be translated integrally and in the most exact manner, without omissions or additions

in terms of their content, and without paraphrases or glosses. Any adaptation to the characteristics or the nature of the various vernacular languages is to be sober and discreet.[1]

When working on *The Roman Missal*, some who provided critique of the translations during the process advocated simply dropping texts because they felt they were too difficult to comprehend. Others felt that texts were simply not able to be comprehended by a younger generation attuned to sound bites and should not be included in the final text. As is evident from the excerpt from LA quoted above, such an approach is simply not workable.

To an already complex task, LA provides a further challenge:

> So that the content of the original texts may be evident and comprehensible even to the faithful who lack any special intellectual formation, the translations should be characterized by a kind of language which is easily understandable, yet which at the same time preserves these texts' dignity, beauty, and doctrinal precision. By means of words of praise and adoration that foster reverence and gratitude in the face of God's majesty, his power, his mercy and his transcendent nature, the translations will respond to the hunger and thirst for the living God that is experienced by the people of our own time, while contributing also to the dignity and beauty of the liturgical celebration itself.[2]

The *Ratio Translationis* is even more specific:

> **The unique style of the Roman rite should be maintained in translation.** By "style" is meant here the distinctive way in which the prayers of the Roman rite are expressed. The principal elements of such a style include a certain conciseness in addressing, praising and entreating God, as well as distinctive syntactical patterns . . . a noble tone, a variety of less complex rhetorical devices, concreteness of images, repetition, parallelism and rhythm as measured through the *cursus*, or ancient standards for stressing syllables of Latin words in prose or poetry.[3]

---

1. *Liturgiam authenticam* (LA), 20.

2. LA, 25.

3. *Ratio Translationis*, 112.

Involvement of the Committee on Divine Worship

LA states very clearly that the translation of the liturgical books into a particular vernacular language, or at least the approval of such books for liturgical use and their printing, remains the responsibility of the Conference of Bishops. This is also indicated in the *Code of Canon Law* in canon 838 §3. This law has its basis in *Sacrosanctum Concilium*, the *Constitution on the Sacred Liturgy*, articles 36–40.

Because of the size of *The Roman Missal* it was decided that ICEL would work on different sections of the Missal and then present those individual sections to the Conferences of Bishops for their approval and ultimately for their vote. It was the decision of the American bishops to review each section as it made its way through the process. The USCCB decided also to submit the various sections to an individual vote by the bishops and then submit that section individually to the CDWDS. In view of the fact that such a careful evaluation was done, this method seems to have worked well. Other Conferences of Bishops decided to wait and submit the entire translation to the CDWDS at the end of the process. What did the process look like for the United States?

The ICEL Episcopal Board reviewed the first draft of a section and, having given its approval, it was sent to the English-speaking Conferences. Because of its cover, this draft was referred to as the Green Book. The Committee on Divine Worship was responsible for making sure that the bishops received the Green Book and were provided with the forms necessary to record their evaluations. ICEL's goal, at this point, was to obtain as many comments and reactions as possible from the bishops and their consultants.

The text of the Order of Mass is a good example of how the process of approval was applied. In August of 2003, ICEL had completed the base text translation and formulated a first draft. Having been approved by the ICEL Episcopal Board in February of 2004, ICEL sent the Green Book to the member Conferences. This was the beginning of the process and so, this first time only, there were actually two Green Books. When the second Green Book was referred back to ICEL there were some 1,175 observations from the United States alone. Here, it is important to remember that since the work of translation was never envisioned as the work of one country, observations came in from all of the English-speaking countries to ICEL.

The Committee on the Liturgy (today called the Committee on Divine Worship) was charged with the dissemination of the Green Book translation to the bishops of the USCCB. Each Bishop was encouraged to review the text with whomever he judged could provide constructive input on the translation. The only limitation was that all observations had to fit within the requirements of LA.

With the help of the Secretariat, the Committee collated the material. It also reviewed the comments of all the bishops and made an executive summary as well as its own observations. All of the material was then returned to ICEL. Bishops also had the opportunity, if they wished, to send their material directly to ICEL for consideration. There were also a few independent groups that provided the bishops with a critique of the text. In some instances, bishops decided to adopt the observations as their own while, in other instances, the observations were simply forwarded to ICEL. ICEL itself had sent out the Green Book to other advisors and translators with specific expertise.

The ICEL Editorial Review Board reviewed the thousands of suggestions that were submitted, and with the help of ICEL translators, a new text was formulated to be submitted to the Episcopal Board of ICEL. With its approval, this final draft, called the Gray Book, was then sent to the Conferences. When a Gray Book arrived at the USCCB it went through a specific process that was shepherded by the Committee on Divine Worship. The text was first sent to all of the bishops along with modification tables. Each of the modifications submitted by the bishops had to be reviewed by the Committee. The modified text was then submitted to the bishops.

Living in the age of electronic communication, a significant decision was made to send the various texts that came from ICEL to the bishops by means of the Web. While this demanded a certain technical familiarity with computers it made a significant impact on the amount of paper used and the cost incurred for printing. If bishops, for some reason, requested a paper copy, it was provided.

By the time of the plenary meeting of the USCCB, the bishops possessed all of the modifications that were accepted or rejected by the Committee. At the meeting itself, the bishops could submit amendments. These amendments were reviewed by the Committee and accepted or declined. If a Bishop disagreed with the Committee's judgment, he could present his amendment to the body of bishops for separate consideration. Such a contested amendment then received discussion by the body. Oftentimes, the discussion raised a variety of issues that were helpful in making a decision about the text. At the conclusion of the discussion, a vote then took place and the amendment was passed or not passed by a simple majority.

After the process of reviewing the amendments was completed, discussion was opened on the entire text of the document. Again, this allowed time for some significant issues to be raised. Finally, the body moved to a vote on the document. According to law, for a liturgical text to pass it must have, at least, a two-thirds majority of the Latin Church members.

Once the Gray Book text was approved by the body of bishops, the Secretariat of Divine Worship prepared the material to be sent to the CDWDS. The necessary materials are indicated by LA; these allow the CDWDS to get a clear idea of the entire context of the translation. A *Relatio of the Proceedings* contains the list of the bishops of the Latin Church in attendance at the plenary meeting at which the document was voted on. Two copies of the action item as it was submitted to the full meeting of the Conference have to be submitted. The final text is then provided. A *Relatio of the Approval* contains the history of the translation of the text as well as the criteria that were applied. A list of the persons participating at various stages of the work, together with a brief note describing the qualifications and expertise of each is provided. The names included are predominantly those from ICEL and the Committee and Secretariat of Divine Worship. Any amendments made to the text or any other adaptations are listed with an explanation of their acceptance by the bishops.

In addition to the hard copies of the text, all of the materials are submitted to the Holy See in electronic files. Finally, after all of this has been prepared, the President of the Conference submits a formal letter to the Prefect of the CDWDS in which he asks for the granting of the *recognitio*.

In February 2006, ICEL submitted the Gray Book version of the Order of Mass. The Committee executed the process which ultimately culminated in the approval of the text with 62 amendments.

The text was then prepared by the then-Secretariat for the Liturgy and submitted to the Holy See for *recognitio*.

When the final text of *The Roman Missal* was received from the Holy See in mid-2010, it was clear that not all of the suggestions made by the USCCB were accepted and integrated. We know that not every Conference obtained the translation of the text as it would have liked to see it completed. But sometimes, it was evident that an American suggestion was accepted. For example, in the Nicene Creed, the USCCB suggested adding the phrase "I believe" at three points to clarify the text and make it more "proclaimable"; the Holy See accepted this change. Elsewhere, in the Proper of Time (formerly the Proper of Seasons), the Conference had difficulties with the word "gibbet" being used in the Collect prayer of the Wednesday of Holy Week; the word was replaced by "yoke." These are but two of the many examples in which the United States' body of bishops collaborated with both ICEL and the Holy See to help produce a text worthy of use in the English-speaking world.

THE CONGREGATION FOR DIVINE WORSHIP AND THE DISCIPLINE OF THE SACRAMENTS

In LA, paragraph 15 notes that the work of translation requires the *recognitio* of the Apostolic See. The *recognitio* for liturgical texts is entrusted to the Congregation for Divine Worship and the Discipline of the Sacraments. This act allows the promulgation of the law of a lower authority. It is not a mere formality but is an absolutely necessary act of the power of governance. This act may also impose modifications—even substantial ones—of the laws or decrees proposed for *recognitio*.

There are many tasks assigned to the CDWDS, but the most important relative to the translation of *The Roman Missal* are 1) the regulation and promotion of the liturgy, primarily the sacraments; 2) the drawing up and revision of liturgical texts; and 3) granting the *recognitio* to translations of liturgical books and their adaptations.

It is this Congregation that was responsible for the development and publication of the *Missale Romanum, editio typica tertia*. There were a significant number of changes that were made since the previous Missal. The CDWDS was responsible for integrating all of these changes into the new Missal. The significant changes were:

Editorial Changes

- Masses for Advent and Easter Time were reordered with one setting for each day, in the same manner as the present English-language Roman Missal.
- Alternative formulæ for various parts of the Order of Mass were inserted in place rather than included in an appendix. Likewise, musical settings for the Order of Mass were included in place.

Additions

- The Prefaces were re-arranged and grouped into five categories: *De Tempore* (Liturgical Times), *Mysteriis Domini* (Feasts and Mysteries of the Lord), *In Festis Sanctorum* (Feasts of the Saints), *In Missis Ritualibus* (In Ritual Masses), and *In Variis Celebrationibus* (In Various Celebrations). Among the new Prefaces was one taken from the Collection of Masses of the Blessed Virgin Mary (*De Maria, forma et matre Ecclesiae*), now found among the votive Masses of the Blessed Virgin Mary. Finally, a second Preface for martyrs is added under the title *De Mirabilis Dei in Martyrum Victoria* (The wonders of God in the victory of the Martyrs).
- The Eucharistic Prayers for Reconciliation and for Various Needs are now found in the Appendix to the Order of Mass.
- Other Prefaces and Mass sets are added from those of *De Ordinatione* and *De Dedicatione Ecclesiæ*, two ritual books whose typical editions appeared subsequent to the 1975 edition of the *Missale Romanum*.
- A Mass setting for each of the scrutinies was provided and two Solemn Blessings are included for the Mass for the Anointing of the Sick.
- Prayers over the People were introduced for each day of Lent in the same manner as the 1962 *Missale Romanum*.
- Mass sets for the Vigils of the Ascension of the Lord and the Epiphany of the Lord were provided and a new extended form of the Vigil Mass for Pentecost was included.

- The complete text of Eucharistic Prayer I was included within the texts of the Evening Mass of the Lord's Supper on Holy Thursday.
- Eight new Masses from the Collection of Masses of the Blessed Virgin Mary were included. Four of these are found in the Common of the Blessed Virgin Mary, while three are found among the Votive Masses: *De Beata Maria, Ecclesiæ Matre* (Blessed Virgin Mary, Mother of the Church), *De Ss. Nomine Mariæ* (The Most Holy Name of Mary), and *De Sancta Maria, Regina Apostolorum* (Most Holy Mary, Queen of the Apostles).
- Among the Masses for Various Needs and Occasions, several new sets have been added, including two Mass formularies restored from the 1962 *Missale Romanum*. The second formulary of the Mass For the Forgiveness of Sins originally bore the title *Ad petendum compunctionem* in 1962, and prays for the gift of sorrow and tears for sin. This Mass is appropriate for use in any circumstance, public or private, in which the need for a contrite heart is sought as a deepening of Christian conversion. The second Mass was originally called *Postulandum continentiam*, and is now the Mass For Chastity; this formulary prays for the grace of self-control, specifically for modesty and chastity as fruits of the Holy Spirit.
- Among the Votive Masses, other new sets have been included under the titles *De Dei Misericordia* (The Mercy of God), *De D.N. Iesu Christo Summo et Aeterno Sacerdote* (Our Lord Jesus Christ, the Eternal High Priest), *De S. Ioanne Baptista* (Saint John the Baptist), and *De Ss. Petro et Paulo, Apostolis* (Saints Peter and Paul, Apostles).
- Eighteen Masses for Saints, newly included in the Universal Calendar, have been added, seven of which are celebrations for recently canonized saints: Saint Adalbert, Bishop and Martyr (April 23), Saint Louis Grignion de Montfort, Priest (April 28), Saint Peter Julian Eymard, Priest (August 2), Saint Peter Claver, Priest (September 9), Saint Lawrence Ruiz and Companions, Martyrs (September 28), Saint Maximilian Mary Kolbe, Priest and Martyr (August 14), Saints Andrew Kim Tae-gŏn, Priest and Paul Chŭng Ha-sang, and Companions, Martyrs (September 20), and Saint Andrew Dũng-Lac, Priest, and Companions, Martyrs (November 24). There are eleven entirely new or restored celebrations: the Most Holy Name of Jesus (January 3), Saint Josephine Bakhita, Virgin (February 8), Our Lady of Fatima

(May 13), Saint Christopher Magallanes, Priest, and Companions, Martyrs (May 21), Saint Rita of Cascia, Religious (May 22), Saint Augustine Zhao Rong, Priest, and Companions, Martyrs (July 9), Saint Apollinaris, Bishop and Martyr (July 20), Saint Sharbel Makhlūf, Priest (July 24), Saint Teresa Benedicta of the Cross, Virgin and Martyr (August 9), the Most Holy Name of Mary (September 12), and Saint Catherine of Alexandria, Virgin and Martyr (November 25).

Emendations

- Emendations have been made to the rubrics for Holy Week (in light of the 1988 *Circular Letter Concerning the Preparation and Celebration of the Easter Feasts*) in the Order of Mass and in the Ritual Masses.
- Some prayers, such as the Collect for the Eighteenth Sunday in Ordinary Time, have been corrected.
- In the Eucharistic Prayers, the intercessions for the Bishop have been emended.
- Antiphons, especially in the Common of the Blessed Virgin Mary and the Common of the Saints, have been brought into conformity with texts used for the same celebrations in the *Graduale Romanum*.
- While in the previous edition of the *Missale*, Masses and Prayers for Various Needs and Occasions were divided into four sections, the present edition divides them into three: *Pro Sancta Ecclesia* (For Holy Church), *Pro Circumstantiis Publicis* (For Civil Needs), and *Ad Diversa* (For Various Occasions).
- In the 1975 edition of the *Missale*, Masses for the Dead were divided into six sections. The revised *Missale Romanum* divides Masses for the Dead into four sections: *In exequias* (Funeral Masses), *In anniversario* (On the Anniversary), *In variis commemorationibus* (Various Commemorations), and *Orationes diversæ pro defunctis* (Various Prayers for the Dead).

Helping the CDWDS in its task of reviewing the translation into English of *The Roman Missal* is the Vox Clara Committee.

Vox Clara

Vox Clara is a committee of senior bishops from Conferences of Bishops throughout the English-speaking world. It was called into existence by the CDWDS on July 19, 2001. This Committee has been chaired by George Cardinal Pell of Sydney, Australia. Justin Cardinal Rigali, Francis Cardinal George, Archbishop Oscar Lipscomb, and Archbishop Alfred Hughes are the American members of this committee. American advisors are Reverend Jeremy Driscoll, OSB, Reverend Dennis McManus, and Monsignor James P. Moroney.

The Committee reviewed the various Green and Gray Books as they were developed and also reviewed all of the suggestions that came from the entire English-speaking world. A report of their work was submitted to the Congregation to aid in its development of the final *recognitio*.

At its meeting of July 17–21, 2006, Vox Clara reviewed the many changes to the text of the Order of Mass submitted not only by the United States but also other English-speaking conferences as well. It then made its final recommendation to the Congregation.

Granting of the *Recognitio*

On June 23, 2008, a letter was sent by Francis Cardinal Arinze in which the *recognitio* was given for the Order of Mass. There had been some discussion about the advisability of granting a partial *recognitio*. As was indicated in the letter from the Congregation, there was a desire to give an impetus to the development of whatever materials were needed to ensure the pastoral preparation of all to receive the new translation. The Congregation made it unequivocally clear that the texts should not be put to use immediately for liturgical celebration. At the same time, the Congregation encouraged the development of musical settings for the various parts of the Mass that had been approved.

In the United States, this provided a special encouragement to both catechetical and musical publishers to prepare catechetical texts for the future. Music publishers developed a two-prong approach. They attempted, where possible, to adapt already existing pieces to the new text. At the same time, they began to encourage musicians to compose new texts that could be used when the Missal was introduced.

At the same time, ICEL gradually brought to completion its work of providing the chants that would be needed for the new Missal. ICEL was most helpful in providing an explanation of its work on its Web site. In addition, an evaluation of the chants was solicited, especially, from the Federation of Diocesan Liturgical Commissions.

As was mentioned earlier, a *recognitio* can also bring with it some substantial changes. Additional formulas for the dismissal of the faithful had been developed and were introduced into the text given to the Conferences. In addition, though not mentioned in the letter from Cardinal Arinze, the translations that were returned had already integrated the decision of the Holy Father that the words of institution should be changed in English to "for many." The CDWDS had already informed the various Conferences of Bishops of the Holy Father's decision in a letter of October 17, 2006.

The CDWDS did not give any indication at that time whether the various sections of *The Roman Missal* would be issued with a separate *recognitio*. Many Conferences of Bishops did not wish the text to be used until such time as the entire Missal was completed.

An example of where a different course of direction was taken was in South Africa. The Southern African Catholic Bishops' Conference decided to go ahead and use the texts of the Order of Mass for liturgical celebrations. There was no catechesis given and that Conference was immediately contacted by the CDWDS and asked to cease implementing the use of the text. Eventually the CDWDS did allow the decision of the bishops to stand but there was a great deal of controversy and confusion among the people, described by some as a revolt.

In March 2010, a formal *recognitio* was given of the final text of the entire Roman Missal. That text went to the publishers at the end of December 2010. Missals will arrive in the parishes in October 2011.

Another important element that the USCCB submitted, along with the Order of Mass, were several adaptations. These were not new, but had existed already in the 1985 edition of *The Sacramentary*, and the bishops wished that they also be included in the new transla-tion. In November 2009, at the plenary meeting of the USCCB, a further group of adaptations were submitted to the CDWDS for integration into the new Missal.

The most recent submission, for example, indicated that in the United States we wished to place in the text for Easter Sunday the renewal of Baptismal promises. This is not in place in the Latin edition of the new Missal. Also submitted was the Proper Calendar for the Dioceses of the United States of America. In addition to the prayers of saints and blesseds celebrated in the United States, there are revised texts for Independence Day and Thanksgiving Day. There are also two new Mass formularies for January 22, a Day of Prayer for the Legal Protection of Unborn Children.

Catechetical Strategy to Introduce the New Edition of *The Roman Missal*

As a result of a meeting between the Secretariat of Divine Worship and publishers of liturgical texts, catechetical books, and music, it became clear that the publishers of the text of *The Roman Missal* would need at least one year to produce the ritual text and have it reach the parishes.

The Committee on Divine Worship decided that the strategy would be a twofold one. The first was a remote catechesis that was underway since the Order of Mass first arrived from the Holy See in mid-2008. At this stage, the goal was to have people become familiar with the texts. Pastors were encouraged to gradually introduce the texts to the faithful in their bulletins and monthly magazines. Catholic newspapers and other media were encouraged to have stories appear about the new translations. The goal, at this stage, was to move beyond the phase of translation questions to the level of unpacking for the faithful the even-greater riches that *The Roman Missal* has to offer with this new translation.

After receiving the *recognitio*, dated March 26, 2010, the Committee quickly met to decide when the implementation date would be. The use of the new edition of *The Roman Missal* begins on the First Sunday of Advent, November 27, 2011. The arrival of the *recognitio* has marked the start of the proximate preparation to receive the Missal, which will last for at least one year, if not longer. This allows time for final formation and for the dissemination of materials. It also allows time for publishers to begin to get their materials to

people. Each English-speaking Conference of Bishops will decide
the date for the use of the new translation in their country.

WEB SITE FOR *THE ROMAN MISSAL* CATECHESIS

Upon the receipt of the *recognitio* of the Order of Mass, the Committee
on Divine Worship wished to encourage and marshal the forces
available to help people to prepare in the time of remote preparation.
The main communications link of the Committee was through its
Newsletter. The changing and shifting aspects of preparing the people
for the new translation needed something that was better adapted to
the communication modes of today.[4]

A preliminary catechetical Web site was launched in August
2008. One year later, in the July 2009 *Newsletter*, it was announced
that the Secretariat of Divine Worship was launching a more expanded
Web site to catechize the priests and the faithful on the forthcoming
edition of *The Roman Missal*. The goal of this site is to offer to priests,
the lay faithful, and worship leaders information that is essential for
the implementation of the translation. A section in Spanish has been
integrated to allow Hispanic Catholics who attended English-language
Masses to learn more about the translations. For those who are
interested, the Web site also presents a broad theological background
for the catechesis. PowerPoint presentations can be found there, along
with bulletin inserts and descriptions of the various liturgical ministries.
The Web site is also used by the Committee as a means to advertise,
support, and encourage the use of the many resources that would be
developed over time.

The Web site is also designed in a special way to allow priests
to prepare for the proclamation of their various parts, including the
Eucharistic Prayers. Priests could, on their own schedule, spend time
reading through the prayers to become familiar with the changes in
vocabulary and cadence. Background material and a bibliography on
the history, content, and development of the Eucharistic Prayer
are included. The site also offers frequently asked questions designed
for people who are extremely busy and cannot navigate through the
entire site.

---

4. The USCCB Web site is www.usccb.org/romanmissal.

Catechetical Resources to Come

USCCB Communications has developed and published a parish guide that will help pastors plan for the implementation of the new translation. This guide provides 1) a planning guide; 2) suggested activities and resources; and 3) a detailed planning workbook for those who may wish to take advantage of the time before the publication of the Missal as a time of liturgical renewal.

The second part of this guide provides an activity suggested for every facet of parish and school life, as well as a calendar of when to do what along with bulletin inserts and homily helps to support the parish catechesis. This guide allows for a pastor to develop a detailed implementation plan that he feels is in accord with the particular character and need of the parish. After the arrival of the *recognitio*, the 12-month planning calendar and some bulletin inserts from the parish guide were posted on *The Roman Missal* Web site.[5]

National Workshops for Clergy and Diocesan Leaders

The USCCB Secretariat of Divine Worship and the Federation of Diocesan Liturgical Commissions (FDLC), with the support of the National Organization for Continuing Education of Roman Catholic Clergy (NOCERCC), developed a series of 20 workshops that were presented throughout the United States in 2010. The core content of these workshops consisted of understanding the background of the new translation, an overview of the new translation, a review of the texts (with a focus on the Order of Mass and the structure and style of the orations), discussion of the *ars celebrandi*, demonstration and practice of the new chants of the Mass, implementation strategies, and a discussion about how to lead a community through change.

The Secretariat led the programs along with speakers from the FDLC. Registration was through the USCCB and the FDLC. It is hoped that those exposed to these workshops began to spread the news after they returned home.

---

5. Please note that Liturgy Training Publications has also developed and launched a Web site devoted to catechetical and spiritual formation and the pastoral implementation of the third edition of *The Roman Missal*. Visit www.RevisedRomanMissal.org for more information.

Obviously twenty or more workshops alone will not be able to meet the needs of everyone who may be interested. It is here that the FDLC has provided resources to be used on the local level.

FDLC RESOURCES

The Federation of Diocesan Liturgical Commissions (FDLC) has provided a resource developed by the dioceses in Illinois and Indiana. It consists of workshops outlined in various manuals. These workshops can be offered for priests, parish life coordinators and parish staff, liturgical ministers, seminarians, and lay people. These resources can be purchased in Microsoft Word and PDF formats.

The FDLC has also developed a number of study papers that will be the foundation for other multimedia materials to be offered. Four study papers were commissioned by the FDLC: "The Liturgical Participation of God's People" by Reverend Mark Francis; "Divining the Vernacular of Ritual Texts" by Reverend Paul Turner; "The Liturgical Implementation of the *Roman Missal*" by Reverend J. M. Foster; and "Liturgical Leadership in a Time of Change" by Bishop Gerald Kicanas of Tucson, then-USCCB Vice President. Begun with a foreword by Bishop Arthur J. Serratelli, eighteenth Chairman of the Committee on Divine Worship (2007–2010), this book, titled *With One Voice*, provides fundamental information that is necessary for one to undertake the task of preparing for the reception of *The Roman Missal*. It can be obtained from USCCB Communications.

Finally, the FDLC developed "boxed workshops" ready to present. The core presentation for the workshops is given by Bishop Arthur J. Serratelli. Some of the topics covered in these workshops are: 1) *Sacrosanctum Concilium*; 2) The structural elements of the 1970 and 2002 Missal; 3) the Art of Presiding; 4) Praying the Prayers of the New Translation; and 5) Leadership in a Time of Change. Individual workshops are available for priests, parish leadership and liturgical ministries, and for the liturgical assembly. In addition, audio recordings, bulletin presentations, and pamphlets are also available, as well as homily hints and suggested methods of implementation of the new translation.

The Leeds Group Formational Materials

Inspired by Bishop Arthur Roche of Leeds, England, an international group of liturgists produced a comprehensive multi-media resource capable of being used by all English-speaking countries for the implementation of the new translation, called *Become One Body, One Spirit in Christ*.

After an introductory video, five sections of content carefully guide users through the new translation. Over eight hours of video are featured, including expert interviews and scenes of Mass from throughout the English-speaking world. Audio demonstrations of the new texts and chants of the Mass, and rich art, architecture, and music from churches around the world complete this valuable resource. *Become One Body, One Spirit in Christ* may be purchased from USCCB Communications.

Beyond the Resources

It seems evident that there will be more than enough resources available for catechetical formation, particularly as publishers begin to release their material. As time goes on and the texts begin to be used, more pastoral and academic texts will appear that will explain the translations and provide people with more extensive background that will allow them to penetrate the deep richness of the new translations.[6]

What is even more necessary now is the willingness of everyone to seize the moment and use it as a special opportunity for a renewed catechesis on the liturgy in general. Every parish, no matter what its limitations, should make some effort to prepare the people for the implementation of the new edition of *The Roman Missal*.

Some Catholics have said that if they only knew then what they know now about the Mass after the Second Vatican Council, the transition would have been much easier. Though we will be adjusting to new translations, there will be a minimal adjustment to ritual this time. This must be an opportunity to once again revisit the liturgical principles of the Second Vatican Council in a deeper and more spiritual manner.

---

6. Visit the Web sites of Liturgy Training Publications for more Missal publications and resources: www.LTP.org and www.RevisedRomanMissal.org.

Once the Missal has been introduced, we will possess a new resource for catechetical formation. Some of the material will, it is hoped, find its way into homilies. Reflections on the new translation might be offered in bulletins. At parish meetings the clergy might take the opportunity of unpacking some of the texts that are found in the new Missal.

For the good of the people and for the peace of the Church, it is imperative that we all develop a positive approach to the task that lies before us. Everyone should be able to find some elements that can be used to deepen the appreciation of the great richness of the prayers in the *The Roman Missal*. Would it not be a tremendous legacy to have it said that never before in the history of the Church had such an extensive and positive catechesis been given on the liturgy? We hope that it will also prepare the next generation to accept the torch from us.

There are moments in history when the opportunity presents itself to take significant steps that can mark a definite turning point. This is the moment that is offered to all of us and it is the hope of the USCCB Committee on Divine Worship that it will be responded to with open and joyous hearts.

Chapter 3

Biblical and Patristic References in the Third Typical Edition of *The Roman Missal*

Reverend Robert L. Tuzik, STL, PHD

For over 40 years, the English-speaking world has used the same basic translation of *The Roman Missal* prepared by the International Commission on English in the Liturgy (ICEL) in the 1960s and 1970s. While it has its weaknesses, it certainly has been an effective instrument in nourishing the faith life of the Catholic English-speaking world during this time. While this article and others preceding it point out the problems with the old translation, we must not forget the context out of which this translation came.

ICEL was founded while the Second Vatican Council was still meeting. At the point where ICEL began its work, we were very new to the task of translating Latin Texts into the vernacular. The main goal of the work of translators was only explained in the most general terms. Today, we have specific norms guiding our translators. The original scholars who worked on the first translations into English did not have this benefit.

In the "Instruction of the Sacred Congregation of Rites on Putting into Effect the Constitution on the Sacred Liturgy," September 26, 1964, you will find the aim of the *Sacrosanctum Concilium* (SC) explained in this fashion:

> But first it must be clearly understood that the aim of the Second Vatican Council's Constitution on the Sacred Liturgy is not simply to bring about changes in the liturgical forms and texts but rather to give inspiration

and encouragement to the instruction of the faithful and the pastoral activity which has the Liturgy for its source and find in the Liturgy the height of its expression (cf. Const., art. 10). Changes which have so far been introduced as well as those which are to be introduced later into the sacred Liturgy have this as their end and object.[1]

What you don't find above, however, are any detailed guidelines about how to achieve this goal in creating the first vernacular translations.

The first guidelines were pretty generic. In Section XI, translation of liturgical texts into the language of the people, in no. 40 of the September 24, 1964, Instruction quoted above, you find this general guideline:

Translations of liturgical texts are to be made from the liturgical Latin. Translations of passages from Scripture must also conform to the liturgical Latin text, although it is always allowed, in order to make the meaning clearer, to have regard to the original or to another translation.[2]

It is clear from the lack of precise directives that the Church had yet to deal with the full challenges involved in producing vernacular translations of *The Roman Missal*.

When ICEL began its work of preparing an English translation of *The Roman Missal*, the words of the *Sacrosanctum Concilium* very much influenced their early work. Especially notable in the works of many of the early liturgical pioneers was their reference to article 14 of SC:

The Church earnestly desires that all the faithful be led to that full, conscious, and active participation in liturgical celebrations called for by the very nature of the liturgy. Such participation by the Christian people as "a chosen race, a royal priesthood, a holy nation, God's own people" (1 Peter 2:9; see 2:4–5) is their right and duty by reason of their baptism.[3]

Based on my contacts with the first English translators of *The Roman Missal*, I believe they saw their task as making the full riches

---

1. *Instruction of the Sacred Congregation of Rites on Putting into Effect the Constitution on the Sacred Liturgy*; found in James J. Megivern's, *Official Catholic Teaching: Worship and Liturgy* (Wilmington, Delaware: McGrath Publishing Company, 1978), page 241.

2. Ibid., page 250.

3. SC, 14.

of the liturgy more accessible to people by providing an easy to understand translation that would allow for "full, conscious, and active participation in the liturgical celebration."[4]

In the May 4, 1967, "Instruction of the Sacred Congregation of Rites on the Correct Implementation of the Constitution on the Sacred Liturgy," there are two paragraphs on the "Use of the Vernacular," which deal mainly with allowing the vernacular to be used in the Canon of the Mass, in all the rites of Holy Orders, and in the lessons of the Divine Office.[5] It was not until January 25, 1969 that the Concilium for the Correct Implementation of the Constitution on the Sacred Liturgy issued *Comme le prévoit: On the Translation of Liturgical Texts for Celebrations with a Congregation.*[6] Unfortunately, by the time this Instruction was issued, most of *The Roman Missal* had already been translated by ICEL and was being submitted to the Bishops' Conferences for final approval, prior to seeking the *recognitio* from Rome.

The January 25, 1969, Instruction, *Comme le prévoit: On the Translation of Liturgical Texts for Celebrations with a Congregation* makes clear the purpose of liturgical translation. It states:

> The purpose of liturgical translation is to proclaim the message of salvation to believers and to express the prayer of the Church to the Lord: "Liturgical translations have become . . . the voice of the Church" (address of Paul VI to participants in the Congress on translations of liturgical texts, 10 November 1965). To achieve this end, it is not sufficient that a liturgical translation merely reproduce the expressions and ideas of the original text. Rather it must faithfully communicate to a given people, and in their own language, that which the Church by means of this given text originally intended to communicate to another people in another time. A faithful translation, therefore, cannot be judged on the basis of individual words: the total context of this specific act of communication must be kept in mind, as well as the literary form proper to the respective language.

> Thus, in the case of liturgical communication, it is necessary to take into account not only the message to be conveyed, but also the speaker, the audience, and the style. Translations, therefore, must be faithful to the art

---

4. Ibid.

5. *Instruction of the Sacred Congregation of Rites on the Correct Implementation of the Constitution on the Sacred Liturgy*; found in Megivern, *op. cit.*, page 307.

6. *Comme le prévoit*, 6.

of communication in all its various aspects, but especially in regard to the message itself, in regard to the audience for which it is intended, and in regard to the manner of expression.[7]

In the passage above, you will find the rationale that motivated the first English translators of *The Roman Missal*. While we may criticize some of the adaptations, additions, and deletions that the original translators made to the Latin text, we should not forget the living context in which they worked, a context where the norms for translation were only published after the translation had been created.

After 40 years of using the text that ICEL initially prepared, we now have a better idea of how to go about the task of translating Latin texts into the vernacular than we had in the 1960s and 1970s when the texts we have been using were first prepared. While I will be pointing out some of the weaknesses of the previous translation, we must never forget that ICEL did the best that it could with a very limited amount of time to produce a vernacular translation with guidelines that were far less precise than those found in *Liturgiam authenticam*.

One of the weaknesses of the previous English translation of *The Roman Missal* is that it often obscured the connections between the prayer text and its source in biblical and patristic writings. This was done in the interest of making the text more understandable and accessible to the people. This approach, however, led to an impoverishment of the English text, with many strong biblical and patristic connections, images, and metaphors weakened or lost.

LITURGIAM AUTHENTICAM

On March 28, 2001, Rome issued an important Instruction, *Liturgiam authenticam*, which provides universal norms for the vernacular translation of the Roman liturgy. In this Instruction, the norms direct translators to strengthen the biblical and patristic connections to the prayers found in *The Roman Missal*.

Characteristic of the orations of the Roman liturgical tradition as well as of the other Catholic Rites is a coherent system of words and patterns of speech, consecrated by the books of Sacred Scripture and by ecclesial

7. Ibid., 7.

tradition, especially the writings of the Fathers of the Church. For this reason the manner of translating the liturgical books should foster a correspondence between the biblical text itself and the liturgical texts of ecclesiastical composition which contain biblical words or allusions. In the translation of such texts, the translator would best be guided by the manner of expression that is characteristic of the version of the Sacred Scriptures approved for liturgical use in the territories for which the translation is being prepared. At the same time, care should be taken to avoid weighting down the text by clumsily over-elaborating the more delicate biblical allusions.[8]

After 40 years of experience in the use of a vernacular text for worship, you find in *Liturgiam authenticam* an approach to translation that more adequately takes into account the important biblical and patristic connections underlying our Roman tradition of liturgical prayer.

BIBLICAL TEXTS

Following the norms of *Liturgiam authenticam*, the revised translation of *The Roman Missal* has made the link to biblical texts more obvious. Nowhere is this more evident than in the opening greetings of the Order of Mass:

> The grace of our Lord Jesus Christ,
> and the love of God,
> and the communion of the Holy Spirit
> be with you all.[9]
> And with your spirit.

> Grace to you and peace from God our Father
> and the Lord Jesus Christ.[10]
> And with your spirit.

> The Lord be with you.[11]
> And with your spirit.

---

8. *Liturgiam authenticam, 49.*

9. See 2 Corinthians 13:13.

10. See Romans 1:7; 1 Corinthians 1:3; 2 Corinthians 1:2; Galatians 1:3; Ephesians 1:2; Philippians 1:2; 2 Thessalonians 1:2; Philemon 1:3.

11. See Judges 6:12; Ruth 2:4; 2 Chronicles 15:2; Luke 1:28; 2 Timothy 4:22.

Much attention has been given to the response: "And with your spirit." The USCCB published an essay on why they changed the response from "And also with you" to "And with your spirit." Let me share with you a few quotes from this essay:

- The response *et cum spiritu tuo* is found in the liturgies of both East and West, from the earliest days of the Church. One of the first instances of its use is found in the *Traditio Apostolica* of Saint Hippolytus, composed in Greek around 215 AD.

- The dialogue is only used between the priest and the people, or exceptionally, between the deacon and the people. The greeting is never used in the Roman liturgy between a non-ordained person and the gathered assembly.

- By greeting the people with the words "The Lord be with you," the priest expresses his desire that the dynamic activity of God's spirit be given to the people of God, enabling them to do the work of transforming the world that God has entrusted to them.

- The expression *et cum spiritu tuo* is only addressed to an ordained minister. Some scholars have suggested that *spiritu* refers to the gift of the spirit he received at ordination. In their response, the people assure the priest of the same divine assistance of God's spirit and, more specifically, help for the priest to use the charismatic gifts given to him in ordination and in so doing to fulfill his prophetic function in the Church.[12]

It is helpful to remember that the biblical uses of the word *spirit* (in Greek, *pneuma*) in the writings of Saint Paul refer to the spiritual part of man that is closest to or most like God. Our spirit is the immediate object of divine influence as well as the place where God dwells. The word *you* simply loses much of the richness of the biblical connections that are maintained when you say, "And with your spirit."

In the first greeting, the phrase "fellowship of the Holy Spirit" has been changed to "communion of the Holy Spirit." This greeting is based on 2 Corinthians 13:13, where Saint Paul uses the Greek word *koinōnia*, which is translated as *communicatio* in the Latin Vulgate. "Communion" is the usual translation for the word *koinōnia*

---

12. The bullet points above are quotes from "Notes on the Translation of the *Missale Romanum, editio typica tertia*" (from the August 2005 BCL Newsletter), "And with your spirit—*et cum spiritu tuo*," available from www.usccb.org/divineworship.

in theological and pastoral works today. Hence, the change from "fellowship" to "communion" is fairly easy to understand.

In a similar fashion, the second option for the Penitential Act is also clearly based on Scripture:

> Have mercy on us, O Lord.
> For we have sinned against you. [13]
>
> Show us, O Lord, your mercy.
> And grant us your salvation. [14]

Unfortunately, this option has not been used as often as it could be in many communities. Perhaps, a greater appreciation for its origins may lead to a better use of these very rich texts.

The Memorial Acclamations may take a little time to get used to, since the revised translation stayed close to the Latin text, which was based on scripture. There were only three acclamations in Latin, despite the fact that the previous translation gave us four acclamations in English. The revised translation of the three acclamations is:

> We proclaim your Death, O Lord,
> and profess your Resurrection
> until you come again. [15]
>
> When we eat this Bread and drink this Cup,
> we proclaim your Death, O Lord,
> until you come again. [16]
>
> Save us, Savior of the world,
> for by your Cross and Resurrection,
> you have set us free. [17]

The revised translation of the acclamations will bring the English translation into accord with translations used in other languages, which more closely adhered to the Latin text than did the previous English translation.

---

13. See Baruch 3:2.
14. See Psalm 85:8.
15. See 1 Corinthians 11:26.
16. See 1 Corinthians 11: 26.
17. See John 4:42.

Prior to the reception of Holy Communion, the priest and people will now say: "Lord, I am not worthy / that you should enter under my roof, / but only say the word / and my soul shall be healed." The previous translation tried to modernize this quote from scripture by eliminating the metaphor "under my roof" and changing "my soul" to "I." The previous translation was: "Lord, I am not worthy to receive you, / but only say the word and I shall be healed."

This is a good example of the approach that ICEL formerly used in translating the Latin text into English. They simplified the text by eliminating metaphors and using pronouns in place of the more spiritual vocabulary ("my soul") found in biblical texts. This prayer is a quote from Luke 7:6–7. In this passage, a Roman Centurion asks Jesus to heal his servant and says to Jesus: "Lord, do not trouble yourself, for I am not worthy to have you come under my roof; therefore I did not presume to come to you" (NRSV). I believe people will find this new translation to be more engaging and spiritually inspiring than the previous translation.

Patristic Texts

While the biblical connections to our prayer texts are fairly well known, the patristic connections are less familiar. Nonetheless, they are an important resource for understanding our Catholic faith. On March 23, 2006, the Papal Master of Ceremonies, Archbishop Pierro Marini, wrote an interesting article, "Returning to the Sources: A Service to the Liturgy." In this article, Archbishop Marini affirms the sources of our Catholic tradition:

- Scripture, the Fathers and the liturgical sources, are not simply testimonies of past history, a subject of archaeological interest, they are testimonials in the deepest sense of the word of a 'story' between God and his people. They are the knots in the woven fabric of which we are the newest threads striving to interlace with one another to form new cloth.
- The Church's labor is precisely this: bringing forth the deeply ingrained new, reshaping an already established deposit. And to do this she must pore over the sources of her faith keeping before her eyes—or better in her heart, the needs of the world today.

- Certainly as we look back we must avoid any sort of archaeologism: the sources do not supply us with pre-packed patterns to repropose. We are not children of a legendary past, instead, believing that the Lord Jesus will come again, we attest that fulfillment lies not behind but ahead of us. Nevertheless we must be wary of flying ahead without roots which would therefore be flying ahead without a goal.[18]

In order to avoid a radical disconnect with the sources of our tradition, it is necessary to examine the patristic roots of the prayers in *The Roman Missal*.

The widely acknowledged dependence of the original four Eucharistic Prayers in English upon patristic sources is a good place to begin our examination of the patristic roots of the prayers in *The Roman Missal*. Each of these Eucharistic Prayers relies heavily upon patristic writings.

Eucharistic Prayer I (Roman Canon), dates from the fourth century (about 378) and is quoted in the treatise, *De Sacramentis*, by Saint Ambrose of Milan. The Roman Canon continued to evolve until the seventh century, when the text became definitively fixed. After the sixteenth century Council of Trent, the Roman Canon was the only Eucharistic Prayer used by the Roman Rite until November 30, 1969, when the new Missal, with its choice of four Eucharistic Prayers, became mandatory. Eucharistic Prayer I has often been praised for its literary beauty and noble simplicity, as well as its strong sense of mystery and awe.

Eucharistic Prayer II is an adaptation of the oldest Eucharistic Prayer on record, found in the *Apostolic Tradition* attributed to Saint Hippolytus (about 215). The English translation of 1969 added the Sanctus, which it did not have, as well as the invocation of the Holy Spirit before the consecration, thus bringing its form into harmony with the norms followed in the other three Eucharistic Prayers. While being the shortest of all the Eucharistic Prayers, it is characterized by clarity, logic, and avoidance of useless repetitions.

---

18. The bullet points above are quotes from Archbishop Pierror Marini, "Returning to the Sources: A Service to the Liturgy," a March 23, 2006, article available from: http://www.vatican.va/news_services/liturgy/2006/documents/ns_lit_doc_20060323_ritorno-fonti_en.html.

Dew of the Holy Spirit

In Eucharistic Prayer II, the restoration of the metaphor, "dew of the Holy Spirit" has been criticized as odd or jarring. The passage reads:

> You are indeed Holy, O Lord,
> the fount of all holiness.
> Make holy, therefore, these gifts, we pray,
> by sending down your Spirit upon them like the dewfall, so that . . . .

The Palestinian origins of this metaphor are more obvious when one recalls how important dew is in the Holy Land during four months of almost rainless summer. Dew becomes a vital source of water, which preserves life in this arid land.

This reference of the "dew of the Spirit" (*ros Spiritus*) has numerous biblical sources, which were pointed out by ICEL in an appendix to the revised Order of Mass:

> The song of the Lord descends from heaven like gentle dew and infuses the faith of humans like grass with a shower of spiritual grace." Ambrose, *Explanatio Psalmorum* xii 5,2. As a figure of speech, it represents abundant fruitfulness (Genesis 27:28), refreshment and renewal (Ps 110:3, Hos 14:5), what is beyond human power (Micah 5:7), and a silent coming (2 Samuel 17:12). But perhaps the most interesting and evocative use of "dew" comes in Isaiah 26:16: "Your dead shall live, their bodies shall rise. O dwellers in the dust, awake and sing for joy! For your dew is a dew of light, and the earth will give birth to those long dead." 'Your' dew here refers to God, not to the dwellers in the dust. The image seems to foreshadow the resurrection of the dead, with the dew of God's light seeping into the darkness of the underworld. This is why it is such a deeply biblical image of the Holy Spirit ("who raised Jesus from the dead"). With its combination of gentleness and power, the image fits well with the working of the Spirit invoked in the epiclesis. [19]

The concept of *ros Spiritus* occurs frequently among Christian Latin writers. Here are some examples:

- Commenting on Psalm 72:6: "May he be like rain (dew) coming down on the fields."

---

19. ICEL Study Notes, *An Appendix to the Order of Mass*, 101.

- "The divine scriptures promised us this rain on the whole earth, to water the world with the dew of the divine Spirit at the coming of the Lord, the Savior."[20]
- "Let the Spirit come like dew, as dew comes and rain. The Lord comes bearing with him rain from heaven, and so we who previously were thirsty now drink, taking inner draughts of that divine Spirit."[21]
- (We must pray for contrition of heart) "that the furnace of our flesh may be extinguished by the dew of the Holy Spirit descending on our hearts."[22]

And so, when the revised translation uses the metaphor "dew of the Spirit," there are some very good reasons why this metaphor was restored to use.

Eucharistic Prayer III is based on a draft for a Eucharistic Prayer that the Vatican Concilium charged with the implementation of the *Constitution on the Sacred Liturgy* had worked on as an alternative to the Roman Canon. Since it is a new composition, it demonstrates better than any of the other Eucharistic Prayers the agreed-upon format that the *General Instruction on the Roman Missal* mandated in all the Eucharistic Prayers. Its emphasis on the action of the Holy Spirit, the sacrificial aspect of the Eucharist, and our participation in the offering of Christ is inspired by themes found in the writings of many of the Church Fathers.

Eucharistic Prayer IV is based on based on the Eastern Church's Anaphora of Saint Basil (about 330). The influence of the Anaphora of Saint Basil is most closely seen in the Preface and the early part of the Eucharistic Prayer, which emphasizes the theme of God's plan of salvation from the creation of Adam to the birth, death, and Resurrection of Christ. It links the eternity of God to the salvation of humankind in a joyous and festive way. At the same time, the revised translation of Eucharistic Prayer IV also takes into account the need for greater inclusivity in its use of passages from the Anaphora of Saint Basil than did the previous translation of this prayer.

---

20. Saint Ambrose, *On the Holy Spirit*, 1, Prol. 8; available from ICEL Study Notes, *An Appendix to the Order of Mass*, 101.

21. Saint Peter Chrysologus, *Sermone*, 60; available from ICEL Study Notes, *An Appendix to the Order of Mass*, 101.

22. Cassian, *Institutes*, 6, 17; available from ICEL Study Notes, *An Appendix to the Order of Mass*, 101.

R*ATIO* T*RANSLATIONIS*

After the Instruction, *Liturgiam authenticam*, was issued in 2001, there were many questions regarding the translation of particular words and phrases referred to in *Liturgicam authenticam*. In order to provide additional guidance for translators and to answer their questions about different ways to translate particular words and phrases, Rome issued a preliminary translation of its Instruction, the *Ratio Translationis* for the English language, in June, 2005, which, after widespread consultation, became final in 2007. In short, the *Ratio Translationis* provides numerous examples of acceptable ways to translate the Latin text into English and further explains the guidelines found in *Liturgiam authenticam*.

The *Ratio Translationis* explains how "liturgical prayer relies upon patristic teaching." It states:

> Prayer texts of the Roman Rite "transmit the faith of the Church as received from the Fathers"—a point that has sometimes been neglected in the translation of liturgical texts. Yet it is crucial that the influence of patristic thought, vocabulary and syntax found in such prayers should be considered by the translator, in conjunction with the biblical foundation upon which such language is often build. Not infrequently, liturgical compositions reflect the way in which biblical revelation was first given expression by the Fathers of the Latin West, especially by Saints Ambrose, Jerome, Augustine, Leo and Gregory.
>
> Many prayers in the *Missale Romanum*, for example, represent a careful synthesis of the mysteries of the Faith, constructed by the Fathers who often articulated their understanding in language borrowed from Western philosophy, though adapted to Christian belief. While the translator's task may be more difficult because of this added dimension, the renewal of the Liturgy is all the more resplendent when the patristic foundations of prayers are place in evidence in the translation. Adherence to "the norm of the Fathers" in the work of translating the Liturgy can thus be considered a key element of the renewal of the Liturgy intended by the Second Vatican Council.[23]

The *Ratio Translationis* provides an example of a prayer that is clearly based on the writings of Pope Leo the Great, in his *Sermo 25*.

---

23. *Ratio Translationis*, 12.

The Latin text of this Sermon is undoubtedly the source of the Collect of the Mass for Christmas Day: "O God, who wondrously created the dignity of human nature and still more wonderfully renewed it, grant, we pray, that we may partake in the divinity of him, who humbled himself to share in our humanity."[24]

The *Ratio Translationis* explains the connections between the Collect of Christmas Day in *The Roman Missal* and Leo's *Sermo 25*:

> Important words and phrases from St. Leo are paralleled in the text of this prayer: (1) the word *substantia*, which is often used in the Vulgate to mean "possessions" or "wealth" (e.g. Gen 15:4, Num 16:32) but sometimes also "existence" (Ps 38:6) or "nature" (Heb 1:3), while it is this latter sense that is corroborated by the context in which St. Leo uses it; and (2) the phrase from St. Leo's sermon, *que et nostrum naturam quam dondidit reformaret*, which characterizes the work of Redemption as a wonderful new act of creation by God. Familiarity with the sources of prayers from the *Missale Romanum* is of fundamental importance in accurate translation, since the meaning of such source texts in their original contexts is often blended into the final form of a collect, preface, antiphon, canticle or blessing.[25]

Unfortunately, the previous translation was not as careful to preserve the connections between the Latin text and its English translation.

SAINT AUGUSTINE (354–430) AND SACRAMENTAL THEOLOGY

One of the Fathers of the Church who has had a major impact both on sacramental theology as well as the composition of many of our prayer texts is Saint Augustine of Hippo. In his famous *Sermon 272*, Augustine says:

> If you wish to be the body of Christ and His members, your mystery lies on the Lord's table, you receive your mystery . . . . For you bear the body

---

24. Ibid.
25. Ibid.

of Christ and you answer: Amen. Be therefore a member of Christ's body in order that your Amen may be true.[26]

This famous passage reminds us that the Eucharist cannot have its full meaning without the mystical body, and the mystical body cannot be complete without the Eucharist.

This passage from Sermon 272 is repeated in part in the Prayer after Communion from the Mass of August 28 for the memorial of Saint Augustine:

> May partaking of Christ's table
> sanctify us, we pray, O Lord,
> that, being made members of his Body,
> we may become what we have received.

In the above example, it is obvious that in order to appreciate the full depth of meaning of this Prayer after Communion, an acknowledgment of its dependence on the writings of Saint Augustine is essential.

References to Scripture and the writings of the Fathers of the Church permeate the prayers of Christmas Time. The famous liturgical theologian, Adrian Nocent, explains these connections in his masterwork, *The Liturgical Year*. Nocent writes:

> The liturgy thus reflects the theology of the Fathers and affirms that our salvation has already been effected in the birth of Christ. Such a statement means, for these writers, that Christ's birth is an intrinsic part of the work of redemption, to the point that it is not simply a condition or indispensable beginning but already contains our deliverance in germ.[27]

In order to appreciate the full depth of the theology captured in the prayers of Christmas Time, a working knowledge of their patristic sources is essential.

---

26. Saint Augustine, *Sermo* 272, quoted in Stanislaus Grabowski, *The Church: An Introduction to the Theology of St. Augustine* (St. Louis, MO: B. Herder Book Co., 1957), page 185, translating the Latin text found in *Patrologia Latina*, ed. J. P. Migne, PL, 38, 1100.

27. Adrian Nocent, *The Liturgical Year, Volume 2* (Collegeville, Minnesota: The Liturgical Press, 1977), page 217.

POPE SAINT LEO THE GREAT (440–61) AND LITURGICAL THEOLOGY

Pope Saint Leo the Great explains the fact that the liturgy makes present the saving event of Christ's Incarnation in his ninth sermon on the Nativity:

[The prophets] teach us not so much to recall the Lord's birth, in which he became flesh, as though it were past, but to gaze upon it as present to us. . . . We retain in the ears of our heart, as though they were spoken at today's celebration, the words of the angel: "I bring you good news of a great joy which will come to all the people; for to you is born this day in the city of David a Savior, who is Christ the Lord."[28]

In order to appreciate the concrete significance of the Incarnation for Christian life today, an awareness of Pope Saint Leo the Great's approach to celebrating the liturgies of Christmas Time is crucial.

Pope Saint Leo the Great is famous for his insistence that salvation is a *present* reality in the celebration of the liturgy. In an often quoted passage extremely important for the theology of liturgy, Pope Saint Leo the Great says:

All that the Son of God did and taught for the reconciliation of the world is not simply known to us through the historical record of the past; we also experience it through the power of his present works. . . . It is not only the courageous, glorious martyrs who share in his suffering: all the faithful who are reborn also share it, and do so in the very act of their rebirth. For when men renounce Satan and believe in God, when they pass from corruption to a new life, when they lay aside the image of the earthly man and take on the form of the heavenly man, they go through a kind of death and resurrection. He who is received by Christ and receives Christ is not the same after his baptism as before; the body of the reborn Christian becomes the flesh of the crucified Christ.[29]

---

28. Ibid., pages 217–218. See Pope Saint Leo the Great, *Sermon 29, 1*, found in *Corpus Christianorum, Series Latina*, 138:146–147.

29. Ibid., Volume 3, pages 173–174. Nocent is quoting Pope Saint Leo the Great's *Sermo 63, 6* found in *Sources Chrétiennes* 74:913.

Hence, you find the rationale behind Pope Saint Leo the Great's most famous quotation: "What was visible in the Lord has passed over into the sacraments."[30]

There is a close link between the events celebrated in the liturgies of Christmas Time and renewal (*renovatio*) of our personal lives of faith. It is as though we, too, were experiencing a new birth (*generatio*) or new life (*novitas*) as a result of our sharing in these sacred mysteries. Pope Saint Leo the Great invites us to thank God, through the Son, in the Holy Spirit, because:

> in his loving mercy he took pity on us, and when we were dead because of sin, he gave us life with Christ so that in Christ we might be a new creation, a new work of his hands. Christians, recognize your true dignity, and now that you have become a sharer in the divine nature, do not return to your earlier degradation through evil ways.[31]

In order to avoid simply turning our Christmas Time liturgies into mere historical memories of past events, we would do well to celebrate the renewal, the new birth, the new life that God offers us at Christmas Time.

Nocent and other scholars find the impact of Pope Saint Leo the Great's teachings in various prayers found in the Masses of Christmas Time. For example, the above quote from Pope Saint Leo the Great's Sermons bears a striking relationship to the sentiments contained in the Prayer After Communion for the Nativity of the Lord, Mass during the Night:

> Grant us, we pray, O Lord our God,
> that we, who are gladdened by participation
> in the feast of our Redeemer's Nativity,
> may through an honorable way of life become worthy of union with him.

In rediscovering the influence of the Fathers of the Church on the prayers of the Roman Rite, you will also find a more dynamic and contemporary approach to the celebration of these sacred mysteries in your own life.

---

30. Ibid., page 218. Nocent is quoting a sermon of Pope Saint Leo the Great that appears in the Office of Readings for Christmas Day.

31. Robert Tuzik, translation.

This dynamic and contemporary approach is evident in the way the Fathers describe the celebration of Christmas as a recreation of the world according to God's original plan. In fact, the Fathers see the event of the Incarnation, of God becoming human, as a way of consecrating the world anew. It is the beginning of a great cosmic renewal for all the created world. The Collect of the Mass during the Day for the Nativity of the Lord hints at these themes when it says:

> O God, who wonderfully created the dignity of human nature
> and still more wonderfully restored it,
> grant, we pray,
> that we may share in the divinity of Christ,
> who humbled himself to share in our humanity.

Without an appreciation for the patristic theology of Christmas Time, the full significance of such a prayer can easily be lost to our modern ears.

SAINT GREGORY OF NYSSA (335–394) AND THE RESTORATION OF THE WORLD ORDER

The idea of restoring and consecrating the world anew is found in a magnificent sermon of Saint Gregory of Nyssa:

> Today the darkness begins to grow shorter and the light to lengthen, as the hours of night become fewer. Nor is it an accident, brothers, that this change occurs on the solemn day when divine life is manifested to men. Rather, to those who are attentive, nature manifests through visible things, a hidden reality. . . . I seem to hear her saying: "Realize, man, as you observe these phenomena, that the invisible is being manifested to you, through the visible. You see, do you not, that night has reached its greatest length, and since it can advance no father, comes to halt and withdraws? Think, then of sin's deadly night that was lengthened by every evil act and had reached its highest pitch of wickedness, but on this day was cut short and allowed to creep no father; it is now being forced to lessen and will finally be completely eliminated. Do you see that the beams of light are more immense and the sun higher than it has been. Realize that the true light is here and, through the rays of the gospel, is illumining the whole earth.[32]

---

32. Adrian Nocent, op. cit., pages 223–224. Nocent is quoting Saint Gregory of Nyssa's work, *Oratio in Diem Natalem Christi*, found in *Patrologia Graeca* 46:1129.

Once again, an awareness of the very rich liturgical theology of the Fathers of the Church can do a great deal in broadening our understanding of the context from which the prayers of our Roman rite have been formed. I encourage the reader to study works such as *The Liturgical Year* by Adrian Nocent, which points out many of the sources for our prayer tradition.

ENTRANCE ANTIPHONS

An often neglected resource that the Church provides for every liturgy is the Entrance Antiphon. These short sentences are often inspired by the great heritage of sermons and biblical commentaries found in the writings of the early Fathers of the Church. They are a treasure house of guidance for entering into the spirit of each day's Eucharistic celebration.

About two-thirds of the Entrance Antiphons are based on Psalm texts.[33] For feasts of the Lord, the Entrance Antiphons correspond to the theme of the feast being celebrated. For other occasions the antiphons are either more generic or else pertain to the season of the year in which they are sung. Sometime they combine quotations from various books of the Bible.

In the late fourth and fifth centuries, the Fathers of the Church (for example, Saints Basil, John Chrysostom, Jerome, Augustine, and Ambrose) wrote a number of commentaries on the Old Testament Psalms.[34] These commentaries influenced the choice of the Entrance Antiphon for many of the Mass texts, which eventually became part of *The Roman Missal*.

What text of the Psalms did they use in the composition of the early antiphons of the Roman Liturgy? One of the most prominent texts came from Saint Jerome, who translated the Old Testament from the original Hebrew, not the Septuagint (Greek text). Saint Jerome corrected the Old Latin psalm texts found in the Roman Psalter around 384 and created a new translation based on the Hebrew text in 400.[35] By the sixth century, Jerome's Vulgate translation began

---

33. Christoph Tietze, *Hymn Introits for the Liturgical Year: The Origin and Early Development of Latin Texts* (Chicago, Illinois: Liturgy Training Publications, Hillenbrand Books, 2005), page 23.

34. Ibid., page 49.

35. Ibid., page 57.

to overtake other texts in local use, becoming the standard translation in Rome after the time of Pope Gregory the Great.

The variety of sources available in the creation of antiphons for the Liturgy of the Hours and for Mass often makes it difficult to trace the origins of individual antiphons. A good example of this is the beautiful antiphon used at Lauds on the solemnity of Mary, the Holy Mother of God. As Adrian Nocent says:

> Research has dated the Latin text as composed at Rome at the end of the sixth or during the seventh century. It is in fact a translation of a troparion that was introduced into the Byzantine liturgy by a poet of the fifth century and is still sung in that liturgy on December 267. The poet in turn was inspired by a sermon that St. Gregory of Nazianzus had preached at Constantinople on January 6, 379, and his composition is a succinct résumé of that sermon. It reads: "Marvelous is the mystery proclaimed today: man's nature is made new as God become man; he remains what he was and becomes what he was not. Yet each nature stays distinct and forever undivided."[36]

In order to appreciate more fully the theology of the two natures of Christ found in the Entrance Antiphon of Lauds for the solemnity of Mary, the Holy Mother of God, it would be helpful to read Saint Gregory of Nazianzus's comments on this solemnity, since they were the inspiration behind this particular antiphon.

The Entrance Antiphons were developed at a time when the commentaries of the Fathers of the Church on scripture were very influential. Since the antiphons often were thematically tied to the mystery celebrated in the particular Mass, the writings of the Fathers on these themes often served as inspiration for the selection of the passage(s) from scripture incorporated into the antiphon. Finally, the influence of the Old Latin translation of scripture and the Latin Vulgate of Saint Jerome need to be considered in order to fully appreciate the sources of the antiphons, which have now been chosen as part of the third edition of *The Roman Missal*.

---

36. Nocent, *The Liturgical Year, Volume 1, op. cit.*, page 204.

FINAL THOUGHTS

Throughout the process of revising the English translation, great care has been taken to restore connections with famous biblical and patristic texts that unfortunately were obscured by the previous translation. In order to do justice to these connections, an entire book could be written on these connections. My hope in writing this essay, however, was simply to point out a few examples of a large number of connections between the prayers of *The Roman Missal* and its biblical and patristic sources. I encourage you to continue pursuing this fascinating study, which opens up the great richness and beauty of the Roman treasury of liturgical prayer.

Chapter 4

The Order of Mass: Comforting Words

Reverend Paul Turner, STL

The Order of Mass is what makes Catholic worship so comfortable. It contains the parts of the Mass that remain the same, day in and day out, from week to week and year to year. Ministers know where to go in what order, what words to say, and what gestures to use. When the priest begins a dialogue, the people know how to respond. The Order of Mass is predictable. Faithful Catholics like it that way.

Changes to the Mass always unbalance the procedures for a while. Catholics grow accustomed to patterns of worship. Part of their piety is going deeper and deeper into words that repeat. Just as someone can read the same scripture passage over and over again and still obtain new insights without getting bored, many parts of the Mass produce a similar effect. Furthermore, the repetition of words and actions supplies the oxygen in which Catholic prayer can breathe. The more the Mass stays the same, the fewer concerns people have, and the more focused their prayer can be. Any change, no matter how slight, can disturb the comfort of Catholic prayer. Once the changes become the new pattern, however, the prayer can retake its deep interior form.

The revised English translation has introduced some changes to the texts in the Order of Mass, the very words that give the Mass its comfortable predictability. Any resistance to change is fundamentally an expression of how important prayer is. It demonstrates a love for the Mass and a desire for the spirituality it is designed to develop. Resistance shows the past success of prayerful words that have written patterns on the heart of a believer. It uncovers the fear that if something changes a little, something else could change a lot. Whenever change comes, resistance is also predictable.

The comforting news about the revised English translation is that it does not change the Order of Mass. It changes the *words* of the Mass, but not the Mass. The Order of Mass currently in force is a fruit of the Spirit-led work of the Second Vatican Council. The *Sacrosanctum Concilium* said, "The Order of Mass is to be revised in a way that will bring out more clearly the intrinsic nature and purpose of its several parts, as also the connection between them, and will more readily achieve the devout, active participation of the faithful."[1] Many revisions took place when the new Order of Mass was unveiled in 1969. The Introductory Rites were simplified. The Liturgy of the Word was expanded. The purpose of the preparation of the gifts became clearer. The number of Eucharistic Prayers grew. The Communion Rite featured more focused prayers for peace. The Concluding Rites were condensed. All of this brought the elements of the Mass into sharper relief individually and totally.

None of that is changing. The vision of the Second Vatican Council is holding firm. The structure of the Mass will still provide worshipers with the comfortable spiritual framework that has engaged them in full, conscious, and active participation.[2] The revision affects the words within that structure.

The words that Catholics speak in English are almost all a translation from originals in Latin, and some from Greek. Those words have evolved across 2000 years of worship. The Lord's Prayer comes from the New Testament. The Preface Dialogue can be found in writings of the third and fourth centuries. Many of the Collects were composed by the sixth century. The private prayers of the priest and the deacon developed during the Middle Ages. The custom of signing the *Book of the Gospels*, the forehead, lips, and heart appeared in the 1570 Missal. The name of Saint Joseph was added to the Roman Canon (Eucharistic Prayer I) in 1962. New Eucharistic Prayers started appearing in 1969, and expanded formulas for the dismissal at the end of Mass were composed in 2008.

---

1. *Sacrosanctum Concilium* (SC), 50.
2. See CSL, 14.

Because these original texts spanned such a vast collection of literature, they have become precious to the Catholic Church's tradition, and they require careful translation. Words that work for one generation may need revising for the next. And words that have been part of the tradition for many centuries deserve to be preserved.

All language groups are undergoing a process of revising their translations of these texts. English-speakers, though, will notice more changes than others will. The original English translation chose a fresh, engaging style that has helped people worship in their own language for the first time with words that resonated with their contemporary culture. This approach, which the Vatican supported at the time, lost some of the nuances embedded in the original Latin. Now the Vatican has challenged translators to keep the prayers understandable in contemporary English, but to plumb more of the meaning from the original. Most other language groups had done this from the start. They had been saying the equivalents of "And with your spirit," "I believe in one God," "He took the chalice," and "Lord, I am not worthy / that you should enter under my roof" ever since 1970. They have prayed the Collects in single sentences. They have said, "through my fault, through my fault, / through my most grievous fault" in the Confiteor. But English-speakers have not. For them, the journey from the first translation to the second is longer than any other language group has to travel. The journey will be difficult, but it will end with translations that reflect the tradition of the Church and unify the voices of Catholics in language groups all over the world.

Overall, people will experience a richer translation than what they have before. The vocabulary has been broadened to match the wide range of words in the original texts. The sentences of many prayers are longer in order to imitate the original style, which is concise yet deep, complex yet meaty. The Eucharistic Prayers will be repeated often as the community cycles through them, and the other presidential prayers that appear annually or seasonally will be repeated on their own cycles. Over time, the repetition of these texts should help people understand them. Once the ears of the faithful adjust to the new styles, they will know what to listen for and how to interiorize the points of liturgical prayer.

Although the overall effect will change the sound and tone of the Mass, many people will be drawn to more minute changes. They will notice how individual words and phrases to which they have become accustomed have been altered. This can be disconcerting, but the revised texts always strive for greater clarity in expressing the Catholic faith. Here are examples of some results from the revised translation of the Order of Mass.

THEOLOGICAL CLARITY

Two words in the revised Nicene Creed are also providing theological clarity. The word "consubstantial" replaces the expression "one in Being." The Latin word *consubstantialis* is difficult to translate because it is so unique. But it describes a unique reality: the relationship between the Father and the Son. The Council of Nicaea labored hard over that word in 325, so the closer the vernacular is to the original, the more faithful it will be to a critical Christian belief. In some English-speaking countries, the word was translated "of one being." Even English-speaking episcopal conferences could not agree on how best to translate *consubstantialis*. For the sake of theological precision, it is probably best to use a word that does not try to interpret further the work of the Church's very first ecumenical council.

A few lines later in the Creed, "was incarnate of the Virgin Mary" replaces "was born of the Virgin Mary." The first English translation could be understood to proclaim that Jesus became human after he was born. But the Incarnation came with his conception. The revised translation makes this clear.

Just before the Eucharistic Prayer, the priest has been asking the people to pray "that our sacrifice may be acceptable." But the revised translation says, "that my sacrifice and yours / may be acceptable." Latin has a perfectly good word for "our," but chose two separate pronouns for this invitation; the revised translation honors this tradition, which has been in place for hundreds of years. Originally the priest was probably alerting the other ministers around him that he was not offering this sacrifice alone; the duty fell to all present. He was probably not trying to distance his sacrifice from anyone else's, but to remind people of their individual responsibility. Through Baptism they are a royal priesthood (1 Peter 2:9), and they exercise that priesthood by offering the sacrifice of themselves at Mass.

Compression and Expansion of Texts

The first English translation contains examples where several Latin words were compressed for ease of comprehension. The practice fit one of the general purposes behind the Vatican's revision of the Order of Mass; namely, to eliminate unnecessary repetitions. For example, multiple Signs of the Cross were removed from the Roman Canon; extra Collects were eliminated from the presidential prayers; the ringing of bells was diminished, as was the striking of the breast. In some instances, the first translators applied the same principle of reduction to the texts. This approach won the Vatican's approval at the time, but today's translators are asked not to make further adaptations beyond what the texts indicate.

The Confiteor supplies one example. The first translation says, "sinned through my own fault," but the revised restores what has always been there in Latin: "greatly sinned. . . through my fault, through my fault, / through my most grievous fault." Other language groups have been saying the Confiteor this way for decades, while the English translation simplified it. Incidentally, prior to the Council the ministers struck their breast three times while saying this line. Ever since the Council everyone is to strike the breast once. The 1969 Order of Mass in Latin simplified the gesture, but not the words that accompany it.

Another example of compressed texts appears in the Gloria. In the opening lines the first translation said, "we worship you, we give you thanks, we praise you for your glory." This, however, compressed a more extensive litany in Latin, which the revised translation reveals: "We praise you, / we bless you, / we adore you, / we glorify you, / we give you thanks for your great glory." Later in the Gloria, the first translation included these two lines once each: "you take away the sin of the world" and "have mercy on us." But those lines appeared twice each in the original Latin, so they have been restored in the revision. Incidentally, the word "sins" instead of "sin" appears in the revised text because the Latin word has been in the plural for hundreds of years. The first English translation put it in the singular. In truth, it appears in the singular in the New Testament, but the Gloria has used the plural form for a very long time.

Sometimes the first translation did the opposite: It expanded a text that was brief. In the Preface Dialogue, for example, the people have concluded with the phrase, "It is right to give him thanks and praise," but the revised translation has, "It is right and just." The first translation was probably expanded to help people understand the nature of the Eucharistic Prayer. Up to this time, worshipers may have followed the Roman Canon in a personal missal, but the priest said the entire text in Latin, in a low voice, while facing the back wall. It was hard for people to follow everything as it was happening. Worshipers generally thought the highlight of the prayer was the elevations, the time when they adored the real presence of Christ in the Eucharist. This was especially true throughout the centuries when the faithful received Communion infrequently. After the Vatican Council the priest started proclaiming the prayer in English in a full voice, facing the people and promoting their engaged participation. The purpose of the entire Eucharistic Prayer is thanksgiving. To help people realize the nature of their role, the first translation of the Preface Dialogue put into their mouths a description of the Eucharistic Prayer: giving God thanks and praise. Today the extra words are unnecessary; people can hear the entire prayer and come to a plainer understanding of its contents and purpose.

This revised response will bring another benefit. The transition from the final line of the dialogue ("It is right and just") to the first line of the Preface ("It is truly right and just") will be smoother.

GENDER-INCLUSIVE LANGUAGE

Many people have objected that the first English translation was not sufficiently sensitive to gender-inclusive language. It can be argued that sensibilities to inclusivity were raised because of that first translation. Up to this point, with Mass in Latin, faithful Catholics were largely unaffected by gender-inclusive issues. Once the Mass went into English, ears were opened, and shortcomings were perceived.

In fact, the Vatican once approved a change to the words of consecration because of gender-exclusive concerns. The very first translation of all the Eucharistic Prayers in the 1970 edition of *The Sacramentary* had the priest hold the chalice and say, "It will be shed for you and for all men so that sins may be forgiven." Objections were raised. When *The Sacramentary* was republished in 1985, the word "men" was removed from this text. There were so many similar passages throughout *The Sacramentary* that it would have been difficult to change them all, but this one received appropriate attention.

The revised translation has taken the opportunity to revisit this issue. The results will not please everyone, but substantial changes have been made because of this sensitive matter. For example, almost all the prayers of the first translation address God as "Father," but the word in Latin is *Deus*, which more literally means "God." Because the new rules for translation want a stronger coherence between Latin and the vernacular languages, almost all the cases where prayers address God as "Father" now carry a more gender-neutral title: God. Exceptions remain wherever the Latin uses the word for "Father," *Pater*, as happens often in Eucharistic Prayer IV, for example.

In many other places, translating more closely what appeared in Latin removes the gender-inclusive concerns. For example, the first English translation of the Collect for December 17 addressed God this way: "creator and redeemer of mankind, you decreed, and your Word became man." But the revised translation, adhering more closely to Latin, advanced with this text: "Creator and Redeemer of human nature, / who willed that your Word should take flesh." In this case, the translators were not explicitly attempting to broaden the gender references; they were simply translating what was there in the first place.

In the Nicene Creed, the masculine pronoun for the Holy Spirit has been replaced with the relative pronoun "who." This became necessary because of the grammatical structure of the Creed, but the result makes the references to the Spirit more gender-neutral.

Still controversial is the word "men" in the Nicene Creed. In the first translation, the faithful were asked to say, "for us men and for our salvation." There has been no change to these words. Many people think the word "men" should be eliminated. The line would be perfectly comprehensible without it, and the omission of the word "men" would alleviate concerns of gender-exclusivity. Many women find it difficult to say the words "for us men." The Nicene Creed, however, draws an important parallel at this point. A few lines later, the Creed states about Jesus Christ that he "became man." The correlation between these two phrases shows that Jesus became what he came to save.

Other languages have been using the same parallelism ever since the Second Vatican Council introduced the vernacular. German has *Für uns Menschen . . . und ist Mensch geworden.* Italian has *Per noi uomini . . . e si è fatto uomo.* French has *Pour nous les hommes . . . et s'est fait home.* And Spanish has *Por nosotros, los hombres . . . y se hizo hombre.* The solution in English will not please everyone, but it does fit an international pattern.

No translation sufficiently captures all the nuances embedded in these lines. To omit "men" eliminates the parallelism. To substitute "human/s" does not quite sound right. Retaining "man/men" offends some worshipers. In the end, the Congregation in Rome thought it was important to keep the parallelism in place, hoping that everyone could take heart in the link between the mysteries of the Incarnation and the redemption.

METAPHORS

The revised translation is restoring some metaphors that were not included in the first one. These were probably omitted because they sound a little strange at first. Examples are "spirit," "soul," "roof," and "dewfall."

Many people are familiar with the classic Latin dialogue between the priest and the people, *Dominus vobiscum. / Et cum spiritu tuo.* There is little dispute over the meaning of the greeting: "The Lord be with you." But the response is another matter. The first English translation rendered it "And also with you," whereas the revised makes it closer to the Latin: "And with your spirit." This dialogue can be traced to the third or fourth century *Apostolic Tradition* and *Apostolic Constitutions.* The people's response is based on the conclusion of four New Testament Epistles (Galatians, Philippians, 2 Timothy and Philemon), where Saint Paul prays that the Lord will be with the spirit of those who read his letter. The word "spirit" probably refers to the guidance of one's thoughts and actions. Today some people charge that the response "And with your spirit" sounds dualistic, as though the body is somehow unworthy of the greeting, but the word is probably just a metaphor. It means "you," but the word "spirit" carries deeper biblical, historical, and liturgical roots. It also sets the tone for the nature of the gathering.

Similarly, in the words preparing for Holy Communion, the first translation had everyone say, "only say the word and I shall be healed," whereas the revised has "only say the word and my soul shall be healed." The words are based on the Roman Centurion's plea that Jesus heal his servant (Matthew 8:8 and Luke 7:6). In the context of Communion, the plea is for the communicant's spiritual healing, not a servant's physical healing. The long liturgical tradition for this prayer has always used the Latin word *anima*. The word "soul" specifies better than the generic "I" the kind of healing people seek in Communion—a spiritual union with Christ.

The same prayer has reinstated another metaphor: "Lord, I am not worthy / that you should enter under my roof" replaces "Lord, I am not worthy to receive you." The same miracle story lies in the background—the Centurion says he is not worthy for Jesus to visit his home. With the first translation, those coming to Holy Communion have been saying a paraphrase, "I am not worthy to receive you," but the restoration of the word "roof" supplies a metaphor that links this communion to the humble request of a believer who trusts in the healing and saving power of Christ.

Eucharistic Prayer II now includes the word "dewfall," a metaphor that was omitted from the first translation. Originally the priest said in English, "Let your Spirit come upon these gifts to make them holy," but now he says, "Make holy, therefore, these gifts, we pray, / by sending down your Spirit upon them like the dewfall." Eucharistic Prayer II is based on an anaphora from the third or fourth century *Apostolic Tradition*. The original had its epiclesis after the Institution narrative, but it was moved forward so that the priest would call for the Spirit before saying the words that the Roman rite holds are consecratory. The post-conciliar revision of this epiclesis imported the word "dewfall" from a seventh or eighth century text in the Gothic Missal. Many different sources have contributed to the Catholic liturgical tradition, and these are represented wherever possible.

The Old Testament frequently employs the metaphor "dew." In Hosea 14:5 the Lord says, "I will be like the dew to Israel," (NRSV) a dew that causes plants to take root and blossom in strength and beauty. In Psalm 133:3, the pleasantness of shared company is compared to dew falling on the mountain, a sign of God's blessing. In Isaiah 45:8, the Lord asks the heavens to bring down the dew of righteousness; this passage inspired the Advent hymn *Rorate, coeli*, which asks the heavens to send forth the Savior like life-giving dew. Of course, biologically, dew does not fall from the sky; it condenses on the ground. Even so, the metaphor does not lose its properties: The community asks for the Holy Spirit to come upon the gifts of bread and wine, that they may take new life and bring the beauty of nourishment. The first English translators probably omitted the metaphor because of the challenge to get it to sound right. But the revised translation hopes that it will inspire reflection among the faithful who pray it.

WORDS OF CONSECRATION

At the heart of the Mass is the Eucharistic Prayer, which is built around the Institution narrative that contains the words of consecration. For Catholics, who believe that Jesus Christ is truly present in the Eucharist, and that the bread and wine become his Body and Blood at the consecration, a change to those words should not be undertaken lightly. The revised translation has joined the task, carefully and prudently, to recast the words of consecration that appear in each of the eucharistic prayers.

These words rely on the accounts of the institution of the Eucharist from four different places in the New Testament. The synoptic accounts of the Gospel relate Jesus' words during the narrative about the Last Supper, and Saint Paul's First Letter to the Corinthians presents them as a response to the way he has heard the community is celebrating the Eucharist. Paul passes on to the next generation of Christians the tradition he learned.

Although the Institution narrative of the Eucharistic Prayer depends on all four of these passages, it does not quote any of them completely. It faithfully passes on the tradition without favoring any one of its streams.

The words are so important to Catholics that only the Pope can authorize a change to them. The revised translation is not creating a new tradition; it is recasting the very same words that have been part of the tradition all along.

"Take this, all of you, and eat of it," the revised text says. The only change is the addition of the word "of." It has always been there in Latin, which is reason enough to include it in the revision, but its appearance now underscores an aspect of this meal. The food is to be shared. People eat of it, a part of it, as members of one community.

"For this is my Body," the revised text says. Here again, only one word is added: "For." It seems unimportant at first, but it connects the thoughts more strongly. The reason the community eats is that this is the Body of Christ.

The same word, "for," appears in the consecration of the wine, where it serves the same purpose. It explains why the community drinks together: This is the Blood of Christ.

"For this is the chalice of my Blood." In the revised translation, "chalice" replaces "cup." The word suggests a liturgical vessel, and it is the word that commonly appears in the Eucharistic Prayers of most other language groups.

"The Blood of the new and eternal covenant" replaces "the blood of the new and everlasting covenant." The word "eternal" suggests a time that cannot be described in terms of how long it lasts.

The words "which will be poured out for you" replace "It will be shed for you." Pouring is a more active verb than shedding, and it implies that Jesus took a willing role in his Passion.

"For you and for many" replaces "For you and for all." This part of the Institution narrative quotes the words of Jesus as recorded by Matthew and Mark. Luke and Paul are silent concerning these words. In both Matthew and Mark, Jesus used the word "many." None of the original sources claims he said "for all." Still, it is clear from many other places in the New Testament that Jesus came for the salvation of all. For example, 1 John 2:2 says that Jesus "is the atoning sacrifice for our sins, and not for ours only, but also for the sins of the whole world." However, in these two instances, the evangelists agree that Jesus used the word "many." Very likely he chose that word as an allusion to Isaiah 53:11–12, which says of the suffering servant, "he bore the sin of many." Jesus probably used this word to let everyone know that he was the suffering servant, the fulfillment of prophecy, the bringer of redemption, and the forgiver of sins.

RUBRICS

Although the primary revisions to the Order of Mass have to do with the words, careful observers will note small changes to the rubrics as well. For example, the first English translation invited the priest to say or sing the Memorial Acclamation together with the people. In practice, the priest joined the people in singing the Amen at the conclusion of the Eucharistic Prayer and the acclamation that follows the Lord's Prayer. These, however, were all designed as dialogues between the priest and the people. The revised translation should draw closer attention to who says what, so that the priest does not respond to words he has just said, and the participating role of the people is strengthened.

The use of the expression "in these or similar words" has also been clarified. The only change in the Order of Mass is in the introduction to the Penitential Act, where the expression appeared in the first translation. The Latin original of the introduction to the Penitential Act, however, never said "in these or similar words," so the expression was not re-introduced in the revised translation. In some other places, although the rubrics have not said "in these or similar words," many priests and deacons have presumed they did; for example, the introduction to the Lord's Prayer, the invitation to extend the Sign of Peace, and the words of dismissal. The rubrics have not changed, but the revised translation may draw more attention to the practice of these parts of the Mass.

These are some of the highlights from the Order of Mass. The revised translation bears scrutiny up close as well as a view from a distance. Like a good painting, the brush strokes tell one story about techniques, and the complete result shows the mastery of the artist. When people appreciate the detail of the work in hand, they come to a greater awareness of the value of the whole.

The revised Order of Mass does not aim to create anything new. It is re-presenting the careful work that liturgical experts completed 40 years earlier to organize the Order of Mass in an intelligible and meaningful way. By taking the same Latin texts the first translators received, the second group has applied new principles, based on insights learned from the preceding work and the experience of praying the texts in English, and have thus fashioned a revised translation of the same material.

It is hard to get a translation that all worshipers find comfortable. Almost everyone will prefer something of the old and something of the new. Worshiping in common does not require preferences in common, but it does require charity in common. Individual Catholics may not like all the words, but they usually like knowing that the words they say are being repeated in every other English-speaking Catholic Church on earth, and that the translation faithfully represents the faith they have received.

The revised Order of Mass may feel awkward at first. But in time it will feel familiar. It should. It is the same Mass. It is based on the same original source. But it has been recast with a new sound that, it is hoped, will invite more profound praise of the God who deserves our prayer from the "rising of the sun to its setting" (Eucharistic Prayer III).

Chapter 5

The Four Eucharistic Prayers of *The Roman Missal*

Monsignor James P. Moroney, STB, STL

The Eucharistic Prayer is "the center and high point of the entire celebration" offered by the priest "in the name of the entire community to God the Father through Jesus Christ in the Holy Spirit."[1] It is the prayer of the whole congregation of the faithful, joined with Christ in confessing the great deeds of God and in the offering of Sacrifice. The *General Instruction of the Roman Missal* (GIRM) describes the parts of very Eucharistic Prayer, which are summarized below.

INTRODUCTORY DIALOGUE

All Eucharistic Prayers begin with an extended introductory dialogue between the priest and the people, which dates from the Fourth Century *Apostolic Tradition* and consists of a series of three acclamations by the priest and responses from the gathered faithful in preparation for the Eucharistic Prayer.

    The new and more precise translation of the dialogue "The Lord be with you" and the response "And with your spirit" has been covered in a previous chapter, consisting of a mutual greetings of priest and people before the beginning of any important liturgical action. This is followed by the priest's call for the people to lift up their hearts, to which they respond that they lift them up to the Lord. Finally, in response to the priest's declaration: "Let us give thanks to the Lord

---

1. GIRM, 78.

our God," the people respond in a closer translation of an old Roman legal formula of approbation: "It is right and just" (*dignum et iustum est*).

The thanksgiving begins with the Preface and continues after the Sanctus (Holy, Holy, Holy). "In the name of the whole of the holy people,"[2] the priest "glorifies God the Father and gives thanks to him for the whole work of salvation or for some particular aspect of it, according to the varying day, festivity, or time of year."[3]

Joined with the heavenly powers, the whole congregation then sings the Sanctus (Holy, Holy, Holy):[4]

Holy, Holy, Holy Lord God of hosts.
Heaven and earth are full of your glory.
Hosanna in the highest.
Blessed is he who comes in the name of the Lord.
Hosanna in the highest.

The epiclesis calls upon the Holy Spirit to consecrate the gifts in order "that the unblemished sacrificial Victim to be consumed in Communion may be for the salvation of those who will partake of it."[5]

The Institution narrative and Consecration consists of the words and actions of the Lord, by which the "Sacrifice is effected which Christ himself instituted during the Last Supper."[6] The Consecration is concluded by the Memorial Acclamation.

The Memorial Acclamation or anamnesis is that prayer by which the Church celebrates the Paschal Mystery, especially Christ's "blessed Passion, glorious Resurrection and Ascension into heaven."[7]

The oblation is that prayer by which the Church offers "the unblemished sacrificial Victim in the Holy Spirit to the Father."[8] Along with the Victim, the faithful offer themselves, so that all might be "that God may at last be all in all."[9]

---

2. GIRM, 79a.
3. GIRM, 79a.
4. Cf. GIRM, 79b.
5. GIRM, 79c.
6. GIRM, 79d.
7. GIRM, 79e.
8. GIRM, 79f.
9. Ibid.

The intercessions, by which the Church on earth prays for the living and the dead.[10]

The concluding doxology glorifies the Triune God and is "affirmed and concluded by the people's acclamation *Amen*."[11] The concluding doxology has been reordered to more closely reflect the trinitarian structure of the Latin text which is prayed through Christ to the almighty Father, in the unity of the Holy Spirit. The previous text reordered the persons of the Trinity from Son-Father-Spirit to Son-Spirit-Father.

CHANGES TO THE TRANSLATION OF THE WORDS OF INSTITUTION AND CONSECRATION AND THE MEMORIAL ACCLAMATIONS

Words of Institution and Consecration

Several changes in the translation of the consecration or Institution narrative have been introduced in each of the Eucharistic Prayers. The changes required the personal approbation of the Holy Father.

> TAKE THIS, ALL OF YOU, AND EAT OF IT,
> FOR THIS IS MY BODY,
> WHICH WILL BE GIVEN UP FOR YOU.
>
> TAKE THIS, ALL OF YOU, AND DRINK FROM IT,
> FOR THIS IS THE CHALICE OF MY BLOOD,
> THE BLOOD OF THE NEW AND ETERNAL COVENANT,
> WHICH WILL BE POURED OUT FOR YOU AND FOR MANY
> FOR THE FORGIVENESS OF SINS.
> DO THIS IN MEMORY OF ME.[12]

Chalice and Cup

The translation of *calix* as chalice, rather than cup, in the words of institution is a noticeable feature of this new translation.

---

10. Cf. GIRM, 79g.

11. GIRM, 79h.

12. The more precise rendering of the Dominical mandate to "eat of" the bread (*ex hoc omnes*) and "drink from" the Chalice (*ex eo omnes*) should be noted along with the translation of the conjunction "for this is my body/the chalice of my blood" (*hoc est enim Corpus meum, hic est enim calix Sanguinis mei*).

There are two words for drinking vessels in Latin: *poculum* is the generic term for any kind of drinking vessel and is customarily translated as "cup." The Latin word *calix*, however, is used more exclusively for a vessel of Communion, destined to be shared with other drinkers. Thus does the Vulgate translate the Greek *poterion* in the Institution narratives in Mark and Luke[13] as *calix* ("chalice"), as a communal dimension is present. Similarly, the liturgical texts have always used *calix* ("chalice") rather than *poculum* ("cup") in the words of Institution and Consecration.

This decision is reinforced by the practice of certain Protestant reformers in intentionally removing the word *chalice* from their translations due to a perceived connection between the word *chalice* and the sacrificial nature of the Mass. A precedent was set for the translation of *calix* as "chalice" in regard to certain translations in the USCCB *Book of the Gospels* and the publication of "The Blessing of a Chalice and Paten."

Poured Out

In the former translation of the words of Institution, the Lord proclaims that his Blood will be "shed." Since the verb *effundetur* refers both to the chalice and to the Blood it contains, however, the translators chose to use the phrase "which will be poured out for you," since "pouring" can be used in reference to either the chalice or the Blood of the Lord.

Pro multis (For Many)

After consulting with the Conferences of Bishops throughout the English-speaking world, Pope Benedict XVI changed the final line of the words of consecration to translate *pro multis* as "*for many*" (1970 = "for all"). The line is a quotation from the words of the Lord at the Last Supper and is found in both Mark 14:24 and Matthew 26:28, where Christ proclaims that his Blood will be poured out. ὑπὲρ πολλῶν and το περι πολλῶν. These passages are appropriately rendered as "for many" in all major modern English-language translations.

---

13. Cf. Mark 14.23; Luke 22.20.

This new and more accurate translation confronts us with the
question: What did the Lord mean when saying that he shed his
Blood "for many"? Why did Jesus not say that he shed his Blood "for
all" in an unambiguous reference to the doctrine of universal salvation?

This question was first asked by the Fathers of the Council of
Trent, who remind us that while Christ shed his Blood for all men,
not all men will necessarily avail themselves of this redemption. In the
words of the *Roman Catechism of the Council of Trent*: "If we look to its
value, we must confess that the Redeemer shed his blood for the
salvation of all; but if we look to the fruit which mankind have received
from it, we shall easily find that it pertains not unto all, but to many
of the human race."[14]

The words of Christ in the consecratory formula, therefore,
refer to the reality actually accepted by individuals: "When therefore
[our Lord] said: 'For you,' he meant those who were present or all
his disciples, with the exception of Judas. When he added, 'and for
many,' he wished to be understood to mean the remainder of the elect
from among the Jews or Gentiles."[15]

THE MYSTERY OF FAITH

One of the more significant changes to the translation of the
Eucharistic Prayers concerns the post-consecration acclamations
introduced by the Priest as he sings or says: "The mystery of faith"
(*Mysterium Fidei*). The declaration "The mystery of faith" is in
response to the consecration that has just been accomplished. It is
a profession of belief in and praise of the Paschal sacrifice by which
the gifts of bread and wine have just been transformed into the Body
and Blood of Christ.

This acclamation is not unlike Saint Paul's recounting of what
has been handed on to him concerning the Lord Jesus' Institution of
the Eucharist,[16] which narrative concludes with the most primitive
form of the first of three responses to the "The mystery of faith" in

---

14. *Roman Catechism of the Council of Trent.*
15. *Roman Catechism of the Council of Trent*, emphasis added.
16. Cf. 1 Corinthians 11:23–27

The Roman Missal: "For as often as you eat this bread and drink the cup, you proclaim the death of the Lord until he comes."[17]

Because the acclamation is in response to the consecration that has just taken place, it is rendered simply by the announcement of what has happened: *The Mystery of Faith* (1970 = "Let us proclaim the Mystery of Faith"), in the same way that the acclamation of the proclaimed word of God is rendered: *The Word of the Lord* (1970 = "This is the Word of the Lord").

The three acclamations are each more precisely rendered, with care given to their suitability for singing. The first two acclamations are inspired by 1 Corinthians 11:26: "For as often as you eat this bread and drink the cup, you proclaim the death of the Lord until he comes."

> We proclaim your Death, O Lord,
> and profess your Resurrection
> until you come again."

> When we eat this Bread and drink this Cup,
> we proclaim your Death, O Lord,
> until you come again."

The third acclamation is inspired by John 4:42: "We no longer believe because of your word; for we have heard for ourselves, and we know that this is truly the savior of the world."

EUCHARISTIC PRAYER I OR ROMAN CANON

It is no exaggeration to say that the Roman Canon, more than any other prayer in our liturgical corpus, has defined the Roman Rite for a millennium and a half. It is, in effect, the *editio typica* of that reality we know as the Roman Catholic Church. Precisely for this reason, the publication of an authentic translation of Roman Canon is among the most significant moments of our generation in the search for an authentic Catholic identity.

Quoted, in part, by Saint Ambrose (337/47–397 AD), the prayer provides a striking emphasis on sacrifice, and the role of the priest in offering it. Scholars trace most of the prayers to the fourth and fifth centuries and believe one of its earliest sources to be the

---

17. 1 Corinthians 11:26.

Syrian Liturgy of Saint James. From the reign of Pope Gregory the Great (590–604 AD), the prayer remained largely unchanged, a practice institutionalized by the post–Tridentine Missal of Pius V (1570). The revisions of the Missal in the liturgical reforms mandated by the Second Vatican Council included a reduction in the number of repetitions and similar modernizations of the prayer.

Eucharistic Prayer I or the Roman Canon may be used on any occasion, although it is particularly appropriate to those days assigned a proper *Communicates*,[18] *Hanc igitur*,[19] or to "celebrations of the Apostles and of the Saints mentioned in the Prayer itself."[20] GIRM, 365 also recommends its use on Sundays.

Te Igitur (Post-Sanctus Thanksgiving)

Rarely does a prayer begin with the word *Te* ("To you"). In the Roman Canon, the use of *Te* at the beginning of the prayer provides a strong sense of orientation, directing the gathered faithful to look to God the Father: "To you, therefore, most merciful Father, we make humble prayer and petition through Jesus Christ, your Son, our Lord."

The new translation makes it immediately clear that the prayer is directed to our "Most merciful Father," through his Son, our Lord, by a humble people. The contrast between God's greatness and our utter dependence on him in our littleness is a common theme of the entire Missal, made clearer by this most recent translation.

Of what does the prayer consist? What does it ask God for? That our merciful Father accept "these gifts, these offerings, / these holy and unblemished sacrifices," given by the people of God and to be offered on their behalf,[21] symbolic of the daily sacrifices the faithful are to offer of their very lives, now joined on this altar to the perfect sacrifice whereby the unblemished Lamb of God is sacrificed for our sins.

As we ask God to accept our "unblemished sacrifices," so we ask him to accept us, his "holy catholic Church," to "grant her peace" (*pacificare*), "guard her" (*custodire*), "unite her" (*adunare*), and "govern

---

18. "In communion with those whose memory we venerate."

19. "Therefore, Lord, we pray."

20. GIRM, 365a.

21. *Rite of Ordination of a Priest*: Presentation of the Chalice and Paten.

her (*regere digneris*) throughout the whole world." It should be noted that former translations habitually referred to the Church in the third person neuter ("it"), while the new rendering always refers to the Church as "she" in order to reflect her spousal relationship with her Lord, Jesus Christ.

The former translation omitted any reference to governance, which is, of course, accomplished through the Pope (who is once again called "your servant," as in the Papal title "servant of the servants of the people of God") and through the Bishop and "all those who, holding to the truth, / hand on the catholic and apostolic faith." This rendering is significantly more precise than the former rendering, since it emphasizes the role of the whole College of Bishops as preserving and handing on what God has revealed to his Church as true.

Memento, Domine

The Roman Canon moves from a prayer for custodians of the faith to a prayer for the Church's "faithful servants." The term *servus* is now translated precisely in order to make clear its original meaning: These servants are the members of the household whom the master will reward upon his return for their faith and devotion.

The *Memento*, it should be noted, is not so much a commemoration of all who are living as a commemoration of the servants who offer "this sacrifice of praise." The somewhat awkward rendering "we offer you this sacrifice of praise / or they offer it for themselves / and all who are dear to them . . ." is an accurate translation of the ancient Latin prayer, reflecting a ninth century interpolation that emphasized the role of the entire gathered liturgical assembly in the offering of the sacrifice.

Why do we offer this sacrifice? The new translation of the *Memento* makes it clear that the purpose of the offering is "the redemption of their souls [the eternal element], / in hope of health and well-being [the temporal element], / and paying their homage to you, / the eternal God, living and true [the liturgical element]."

Communicantes

The new translation recognizes the full context of the *Communicantes*: having prayed in communion with the saints on earth in the previous paragraph, we now pray in communion with the saints in heaven, "whose memory we venerate." The full Latin title for the Mother of God is now translated: "the glorious ever-Virgin Mary, / Mother of our God and Lord, Jesus Christ." The titles of blessed (*beatus*) Joseph and the introductory title to the whole list of saints: blessed (*beautus*) Apostles and Martyrs is also translated for the first time. Finally, it is not simply by the prayers of the saints, but by "their merits and prayers" that God is asked to grant us his "protecting help" (1970 = "help and protection").

Hanc Igitur

The *Hanc igitur*, begins with a more precise rendering of the Latin address of God as Lord, rather than Father, along with the request that God accept this "oblation of our service" (1970 = "offering"). Entirely missing from the former translation is the description of the offerers as "your whole family," a phrase similar to that found in the *Memento*, above. Three petitions are then presented to God. The first ("order our days in your peace"), attributed to Pope Gregory the Great, is precisely translated for the first time, along with the pastoral imagery of the phrase, "command that we be delivered from eternal damnation / and counted among the flock of those you have chosen."

Quam oblationem (Epiclesis)

The epiclesis follows, in which the former translation omitted the petition that God acknowledge (*adscriptam*) in the phrase "bless, acknowledge, / and approve this offering in every respect . . . ." The somewhat difficult phrase *rationabilis acceptabilemque*, is now more precisely rendered as "make it spiritual and acceptable," restoring to the text its clearly sacrificial character.[22]

Qui pridie (Words of Institution and Consecration)

Here, typically, where the former translation conflated sacralizing adjectives ("holy" and "venerable" = "sacred"), the new translation renders them more fully. Likewise, "with eyes raised to heaven" was previously rendered by the less precise "looking up to heaven" and the

---

22. Cf. Malachi 1:11.

former "giving you thanks, he said the blessing," as "giving you thanks and praise" in the consecration of both elements.

The *Missale Romanum*'s traditional introductory phrase for the consecration of the chalice ("In a similar way") is no longer omitted in any of the Eucharistic Prayers. The introduction to the words of consecration spoken over the chalice is also more precisely translated, as "cup" becomes "this precious chalice" and "in his holy and venerable hands" is translated for the first time.

Unde et memores (**Memorial**)

The rather vague connotations of the prior translation (1970 = "the memory of Christ, your Son") are replaced with a more precise proclamation of our celebration of "the memorial of the blessed Passion, / the Resurrection from the dead, / and the glorious Ascension into heaven / of Christ, your Son, our Lord . . . ." The rather flat "your people and your ministers" is now accurately rendered as "your servants and your holy people."

The new and more precise translation of the next five lines describe what is being offered: "this pure victim, this holy victim, this spotless victim, the holy bread of eternal life[23] and the Chalice of everlasting salvation."[24] The former translation condensed and simplified the content of these lines as "this holy and perfect sacrifice: the bread of life and the cup of eternal salvation." This all results in a significantly richer and broader description of the Holy Eucharist. This is not just a holy and perfect sacrifice, but a pure, holy, and spotless victim: the unblemished Paschal lamb who takes upon himself the sins of the world. It is not just the bread of life, but the bread of eternal life, for he who eats the Body of the Lord will never really die.

The rather long petition, "Be pleased to look upon these offerings / with a serene and kindly countenance . . ." was rendered by the phrase "Look with favor" in the prior translation. Two words are used to describe the way in which we ask God to look upon our sacrifice: *propitio ac sereno*. *Propitio* clearly means kindly, while many words were suggested for *sereno*, a word that translators suggested means

---

23. Cf. John 6:35, 48.
24. Cf. Psalm 116:13.

both untroubled and untroubling. In the end, serene, although some-what uncommon today, was judged to be the most appropriate choice.

Supra quæ propitio

The three classical Old Testament types of the sacrifice of the Eucharist are then referenced: Abel,[25] Abraham,[26] and Melchizedek.[27] Abel's title (Abel the just) is restored, and the simplification and unwarranted specification of the offering of Melchizedek (1970 = "the bread and wine offered by your priest Melchizedek") is corrected with: "the offering of your high priest Melchizedek, / a holy sacrifice, a spotless victim."

*Supplices te rogamu*s

The only prayer of the Eucharistic Prayers accompanied by a profound bow is intended to express our unworthiness in begging for God to unite this sacrifice with the heavenly banquet. Where the former translation failed to translate words like "humble prayer . . . command . . . borne by the hands of your holy . . . in the sight of your divine majesty . . . heavenly blessing" it failed to sufficiently to reflect this articulation of our littleness and God's majesty. Likewise, the prior translation's reduction of participation at the altar to a simple reception of Holy Communion has been remedied.

Memento etiam (Commemoration of the Dead)

In the commemoration of the faithful departed, the Latin text is now more precisely translated in praying for the Lord's "servants" and not just "those who have died" with the sign of faith. The curious omis-sion of a reference to *sic* as those who "rest in the sleep of peace," has been rectified.

The commemoration of the dead concludes with a prayer that all who sleep in Christ will be granted a place of *dormire, somnum,* and *quiescere.* The translators correctly noted that all three words are close in meaning and present particular challenges for translating into

---

25. Cf. Genesis 4:4.
26. Cf. Genesis 15:7–21; 22:13; Romans 4:11.
27. Cf. Genesis 14:18–20.

English. "Refreshment, light, and peace" were chosen as somewhat traditional in English language translations.

Nobis quoque peccatoribus (Commemoration of the Living)

The final petition for the Church ("To us, also, your servants") restores the reference to us as God's servants, concluding with the more precise translation by which the priest prays, while striking his breast, "admit us, we beseech you, into their company, not weighing our merits, but granting us your pardon."

For the doxology, see discussion above.

EUCHARISTIC PRAYER II

Eucharistic Prayer II is the shortest of the Eucharistic Prayers and is based on a fourth century text from the *Apostolic Tradition*. Eucharistic Prayer II is most appropriate on weekdays and in special circumstances.[28]

Preface

The Preface which may be replaced with any of the other Prefaces of the Missal, "especially those which sum up the mystery of salvation, for example, the Common Prefaces,"[29] emphasizes the saving role of the Son of God, through whom the Father made the universe (1970 = "all things") and who was sent from the Father as our Savior and Redeemer. The former translation avoids these titles and describes the Son as "the Savior you sent to redeem us." As in the new rendering of the Creed, Christ is described as incarnate by the Holy Spirit and born of the Virgin Mary.

The prayer then recalls how Christ accepted his Passion, in fulfillment of the Father's will, choosing to use the more traditional word "Passion" rather than the former translation's "suffering." In a more poetic rendering the prayer recalls how the Lord "stretched out his hands as he endured his Passion" (1970 = "he opened his arms on the cross").

---

28. GIRM, 365b.
29. GIRM, 365b.

Post-Sanctus Thanksgiving

Following the Sanctus, the prayer continues with a two line introduction, echoing the Sanctus and recalling that God is the *fountain* of all holiness. The epiclesis is little changed from the prior translation with the exception of a more accurate translation of *spiritus tui rore sanctifica* = "sending down your Spirit upon them like the dewfall."

Epiclesis

"Dewfall" here recalls a number of complex scriptural allusions, first to the manna which descended upon the Israelites in the desert "when the dew fell upon the camp . . . ."[30] This manna was a foreshadowing of the Holy Eucharist, as the Lord tells us in the Gospel according to John: "Your ancestors ate the manna in the desert, but they died; this is the bread that comes down from heaven so that one may eat it and not die."[31]

Thus does the epiclesis ask that, like the manna with which he fed the Israelites in the wilderness, the Holy Spirit might descend upon these offerings like the dewfall and "that they might become for us the Body and Blood of our Lord, Jesus Christ."

While the changes in the words of consecration and the mystery of faith are addressed above, the thanksgiving follows. Here a closer translation highlights the scriptural allusions of the text ("Bread of Life, Chalice of Salvation") rather than interpreting these phrases ("life-giving bread, saving cup") as in the prior translation.

Intercession for the Living

The intercession for the living asks simply that by sharing in Christ's Body and Blood, the Church spread throughout the world might be gathered into one, brought to the fullness of charity[32] through the Pope and the clergy.

In the light of significant pastoral objections to a too literal translation of *dignos habuisti astare coram* leading to an exclusion of those who may be kneeling at this point in the Mass, the phrase

---

30. Numbers 11:9.

31. John 6:49–50.

32. 1 John 4:18.

has been rendered as "held us worthy / to be in your presence and minister to you."

Deprecatory language has been restored throughout the Eucharistic Prayers, as exemplified by this intercession, which now begins with the phrase "Humbly we pray . . ." Similarly, the phrase "your Church, throughout the world" is now "your Church, / spread throughout the world."

Intercession for the Dead[33]

In the memorial of the dead, the scriptural sense of Romans 6:5[34] is brought out more clearly than the previous translation: "that he (she) who was united with your Son in a death like his, / may also be one with him in his Resurrection."

The ancient language of the prayers is likewise restored in the alternative intercession for the dead, which asks the Lord to remember those "who have fallen asleep" (rather than, "gone to their rest") and "the hope of the resurrection" (rather than "the hope of rising again." Finally, here and throughout the revised Missal, traditional titles are translated for "the blessed Virgin Mary" and the "blessed Apostles." A more precise rendering of the saints as those "who have pleased you" replaced the simple those "who have done your will."

EUCHARISTIC PRAYER III

Eucharistic Prayer III is an entirely modern composition that may be used with any Preface from the Missal and is most appropriate for Sundays and festive days.[35]

Introduction

The introduction echoes the Sanctus proclamation of the holiness of the Lord and how all God has created gives him praise. The prior

---

33. "For if we have been united with him in a death like his, we will certainly be united with him in a resurrection like his." *Complantatus* in this text translates Greek *sumphutos*, used to express similarity between things, like the similarity of plants planted in a row. Since the underlying agricultural metaphor appears already to have faded by Plato's time (see Liddell and Scott, sv), it seemed unnecessary to reproduce it here. See paragraph 115 of the liturgical text.

34. "For if we have grown into union with him through a death like his, we shall also be united with him in the resurrection."

35. Cf. GIRM, 365c.

rendering failed to make clear that God is the author of all the creatures who now praise him.

That praise of the Father is through Jesus Christ, his Son, "by the power and working of the Holy Spirit." While creation praises its creator, he continues to manifest his love by making all things holy, never ceasing to gather a people to himself "so that from the rising of the sun to its setting / a pure sacrifice may be offered" to his name.

In the prior translation a geographical reference (1970 = "from East to West") was used, but failed to sufficiently echo the passage from the prophet Malachi that inspired this paragraph: "For from the rising of the sun to its setting my name is great among the nations, and in every place incense is offered to my name, and a pure offering; for my name is great among the nations, says the Lord of hosts."[36]

Epiclesis

The epiclesis begins with a deprecatory phrase ("we humbly implore you") omitted in the previous rendering and asks that the same Spirit "graciously make holy / these gifts we have brought to you for consecration" that they may become the Body and Blood of the Lord "at whose command we celebrate these mysteries." ("These mysteries" was interpreted as "this Eucharist" in the 1970 rendering).

The Epiclesis continues with the traditional phrase "as we celebrate the memorial" (prior translation = "calling to mind") of the saving Passion, Resurrection, and Ascension into heaven, "we look forward to his second coming" (prior = "ready to greet him when he comes again") and uses the typical phrase "we offer you in thanksgiving this holy and living sacrifice." Finally, God is asked to look upon the Church's oblation (prior = "offering") and recognize ("see") the Victim who is our reconciliation and our nourishment as the Holy Spirit makes "one body and one spirit in Christ"; thus, may Christ "make of us an eternal offering (gift) to you."

This making of all as one is particularly accented by our unity with the Virgin Mary, Apostles, martyrs, and patron or saint of the day. As elsewhere, the titles of the Virgin Mary and the Saints are restored in the new translation. This paragraph concludes with a reflection on our relationship with the saints as those on whose

---

36. Malachi 1:1.

constant intercession and unfailing help we rely. That this intercession takes place in the realm of the blessed is conveyed by the newly translated phrase "constant intercession in your presence."

Traditional vocabulary is again more precisely translated in referring to "this Sacrifice of our reconciliation" rather than "this sacrifice, which has made our peace with you." We then pray that the sacrifice might advance the peace and salutation of all the world and that God might "be pleased to confirm in faith and charity" his Pilgrim Church on earth (contrasted with the intercession of the saints in heaven) with the Pope, the Bishops, "the Order of Bishops" ("all the bishops") and all the clergy, and "the entire people you have gained for your own."

God is then asked to listen graciously to the family he has summoned before him: "in your compassion (mercy and love) O merciful Father, gather to yourself (unite) all your children scattered throughout the world (wherever they may be)."

The commemoration of the dead prays for two groups: "our departed brothers and sisters" and "all who were pleasing to you at their passing from this life." We ask God to give both "kind admittance to your kingdom."

The transition to the doxology is set within the context of the heavenly kingdom, where "we hope to enjoy for ever the fullness [vision] of your glory / through Christ our Lord, / through whom you bestow on the world all that is good (from whom all good things come)."

Eucharistic Prayer IV

Eucharistic Prayer IV is based on several Eastern sources and is the longest of the Roman Eucharistic Prayers. Structured as a recounting of the history of salvation, the Eucharistic Prayer has an unchangeable Preface and may be used on Sundays, but not on those feasts when a proper Preface is provided.[37]

Preface

The Preface is the longest of all the Eucharistic Prayers and recounts the holiness of God, his creation of the world, and his sustaining will that all men be saved.

37. Cf. GIRM, 365d.

Many of the changes to the translation of the fourth Eucharistic Prayer are stylistic, reflecting the highly poetic style of this text. The newer rendering reflects more closely the poetic expressions and syntax of the Latin. For example, the more ornate, "existing before all ages and abiding for all eternity, / dwelling in unapproachable light," was previously rendered, "Through all eternity you live in unapproachable light."

The prayer continues to recall that it is God "who alone are good, the source of life, / have made all that is . . . ." He wills every creature with blessings, brings joy to many of them "by the glory of [his] light." The prior translation erroneously implied that "all men" were brought to the glory of God's light.

The Preface concludes typically by recalling the angels, "who serve you day and night . . . gazing on the glory of your face." We, too, "confess your name in exultation, / giving voice to every creature under heaven, / as we acclaim."

Post-Sanctus Thanksgiving

The post-Sanctus introduction is an extended thanksgiving for the salvation history, recounting the wonderful works of God in guiding his people in the ways of holiness and truth. As with all the Eucharistic Prayers, it begins by echoing the Sanctus: "We give you praise," a more precise translation than previously (1970 = "we acknowledge your greatness"). God is addressed as "Father most holy" (1970 = "Father").

God is then thanked for forming man in his own image (previous = "likeness") and entrusting him with the whole world for service of God and dominion over all creatures.

The next paragraph then recalls the fall, whereby man "lost your friendship," recalling that God did not than abandon mankind "to the domain (1970 = "power") of death." Recalling God's fidelity to the chosen people, the prayer then recalls how God "came in mercy to the aid of all, / so that those who seek might find you." This more precise translation of the Latin avoids the implications of the previous translation, "helped all men to seek and find you."

The Latin text then declares that God had "time and again" offered covenants to man and taught him to look forward to salvation. The previous translation rendered covenant in the singular. While it is true that God's covenant with the chosen people is singular, the prayer here refers to the alliances that God swore with Abraham, Moses, David, and so on.

The next paragraph repeats the title "Father most holy," and recalls the "Incarnation of your Only Begotten Son to be our Savior." Recalling the usage of the Creed, he is "Incarnate by the Holy Spirit and born of the Virgin Mary." The over read of the previous translation (1970 = "a man like us in all things but sin") is replaced by a more precise reading: "he shared our human nature in all things but sin."

Christ's proclamation of the Good News of the Kingdom of God is then recalled, listing those to whom he preached: the poor, prisoners, and the sorrowful of heart (1970 = "those in sorrow.") The content of the proclamation is matched to the condition of the recipient in each instance ("poor . . . good news of salvation; prisoners . . . freedom; sorrowful of heart . . . joy").

This recounting of salvation history concludes with the Paschal Mystery, whereby: "to accomplish your plan" Christ "gave himself up to death, and, rising from the dead, / he destroyed death and restored life."

Epiclesis

The Epiclesis is a continuation of the narrative of the previous section, now describing our participation in the story. In order that "we might live no longer for ourselves, / but for him who died and rose again for us," Christ sends the Holy Spirit from the Father as the "first fruits" of our salvation, in order that his work might be completed and creation might be fully sanctified. The epiclesis then asks that "this same Holy Spirit / graciously sanctify these gifts" that they might become Christ's Body and Blood for us.

Post-Sanctus Memorial

The memorial then recalls "Christ's Death / and his descent to the realm of the dead." The Latin term here is clearly describing hell as an actual place, as opposed to the prior translation's more vague "descent among the dead." This is followed by a proclamation of the Resurrection and Ascension "to your right hand," and "we offer you his Body and

Blood, / the sacrifice acceptable to you (1970 = "the acceptable sacrifice") / which brings salvation to the whole world."

The prayer then intercedes that God look upon the sacrifice that he has provided for his Church and gather all who partake of "this one Bread and one Chalice" into one body by the Holy Spirit, that they "may truly become a living sacrifice in Christ / to the praise of your glory."

Commemoration of the Living

This petition for unity is followed by a prayer for those "for whom we offer this sacrifice," especially the Pope, the Bishop, the Order of Bishops, the clergy , "those who take part in this offering, / those gathered here before you, / your entire people, / and all who seek you with a sincere heart."

Commemoration of the Dead

The intercession for the dead is the simplest of all the Eucharistic Prayers, simply asking God to remember "those who have died in the peace of your Christ / and all the dead, / whose faith you alone have known."

Transition to the Doxology

The prayer concludes with a petition for "us, your children" that we might "enter into a heavenly inheritance" with the blessed Virgin, the Apostles and the Saints, in that place where "with the whole of creation (1970 = "every creature"), freed from the corruption of sin and death, / may we glorify you through Christ our Lord, / through whom you bestow on the world (1970 = "give us") all that is good."

CONCLUSION

This brief review of the Eucharistic Prayers of *The Roman Missal* is but a first small step in realizing the opportunity we now have to renew the liturgy and the Church. Only through a continuing focused study of the theological meaning of the Eucharistic Prayers in their proper historical and ecclesial contexts will they become accessible and nourishing for the life of the Church in each parish celebration of the Sacred Liturgy.

Indeed, there is no pastoral endeavor more fruitful, and no initiative more worthwhile than to seek that full, conscious, and active participation in the source and the summit of the Christian life first envisioned by the Council Fathers almost a half century ago.

Chapter 6

Eucharistic Prayers for Reconciliation

Reverend Ronald T. Kunkel, STB, STL, STD (candidate)

Although the twentieth century witnessed many technological developments and scientific advances that have benefitted the human community, the historical period is perhaps most notable for the staggering loss of life and degree of suffering that resulted from wars, terrorism, and various other affronts to the dignity of the human person. From the carnage of World War I to the atrocities committed under Hitler and Stalin, from the Killing Fields of Cambodia to ethnic cleansing in the Balkans, there were many serious wounds inflicted on the family of humankind.

Of all these, one of the most tragic occurred in the African nation of Rwanda. In 1994, an estimated 800,000 people, representing about 20 percent of the country's population, were slaughtered in genocidal mass killings perpetrated by the Hutu-dominated government. Men, women, and children of the rival Tutsi tribe, as well as moderates within the Hutus, were massacred, often in especially brutal ways. A further heartbreaking aspect of this tragedy lies in the fact that Rwanda is an overwhelmingly Christian country, with a majority of the population belonging to the Catholic Church. Yet even in these most difficult and painful of circumstances, seeds of hope emerge. In 2008, the filmmaker Laura Waters Hinson produced an award-winning documentary entitled *As We Forgive*, which depicts actual encounters between survivors of the Rwandan genocide and those who participated in these acts of violence. The film demonstrates that the only way forward, for the involved persons themselves as well as the nation as a whole, is the long, painful, yet ultimately healing path of reconciliation.

RECONCILIATION IN THE GOSPEL AND THE LIFE OF THE CHURCH

Reconciliation, the act of being restored to friendship or harmony, is at the heart of the Christian faith. It permeates the pages of the Bible and the literature of the Church, under the term itself or many others that touch upon the same reality, for instance, salvation, satisfaction, justification, forgiveness, redemption, or liberation. Reconciliation reflects the restoration of communion between sinful human beings and the God of love and mercy, as well as the renewal of the relationships among the members of the community. The New Testament reveals Jesus Christ as the one in whom reconciliation is definitively achieved and perfected. Paul asserts: "For if while we were enemies, we were reconciled to God through the death of his Son, much more surely, having been reconciled, will we be saved by his life."[1]

Through the Paschal Mystery of the Lord's Passion, Death, Resurrection, and glorification, the world is reconciled to God the Father, through Christ his Son, in the Holy Spirit. This ministry of reconciliation has been entrusted by Jesus to the Church[2] and is celebrated in her work of *martyria* (witness), *diakonia* (service), and *leitourgia* (worship). Wherever the Gospel is preached and witnessed to, in whatever form works of Christian charity and service are performed for the good of the human family around the world, and whenever the Church celebrates the Sacred Liturgy and so enables us to participate in the mysteries of our redemption, the ministry of reconciliation effected in the person of Jesus Christ continues to bear fruit through his Body, the Church, "the universal sacrament of salvation."[3] As Pope John Paul II proclaimed:

> We experience the reconciliation which he accomplished in his humanity in the efficacy of the sacred mysteries which are celebrated by his church, for which he gave his life and which he established as the sign and also the means of salvation.[4]

---

1. Romans 5:10, NRSV.

2. Cf. Matthew 16:18–19, 18:18, 28:19–20; John 20:19–23; 2 Corinthians 5:18–20.

3. *Lumen Gentium*, 48.

4. *Reconciliatio et Paenetentia*, 8.

Reconciliation, in the truest sense, is thus accomplished in the liturgical-sacramental life of the Church. Forgiveness of sins and reconciliation with God and the Church begins through the waters of the Sacrament of Baptism, as we are washed clean and incorporated as members of Christ's ecclesial body.

Those who rupture their communion with God and the community through serious sins after Baptism are renewed and restored by the Sacrament of Penance, or Reconciliation, which restores one to friendship with the Lord and reintegrates one into full participation at the banquet of the Eucharist. Persons who are burdened by serious illness are united to the mystery of the Lord's Cross and given the grace of healing, including the forgiveness of sins, through the Sacrament of the Anointing of the Sick. From week to week, however, and even from day to day, it is the celebration of the Eucharist that manifests most clearly the Church as the sign and instrument of reconciliation for the world.

As the source and summit of the Christian life and of every dimension of the Church's mission and activity[5], the Church proclaims:

> The Eucharist is the efficacious sign and sublime cause of that communion in the divine life and that unity of the People of God by which the Church is kept in being. It is the culmination both of God's action sanctifying the world in Christ and of the worship men offer to Christ and through him to the Father in the Holy Spirit.[6]

As John Paul II wrote simply yet so profoundly, "The Church draws her life from the Eucharist."[7] The life of the Church is rooted in its reality as a reconciled community of faith, whose mission is to bring about the reconciliation of the entire world. The Eucharist is both the source and the goal of the ecclesial work of reconciliation.

---

5. Cf. *Sacrosanctum Concilium*, 10; *Lumen Gentium*, 11; *Presbyterorum Ordinis*, 5.

6. *Catechism of the Catholic Church* (CCC), 1325, quoting Instruction of Sacred Congregation for Rites, *Eucharisticum mysterium*, 6.

7. *Ecclesia de Eucharistia*, 1.

RECONCILIATION IN THE EUCHARISTIC PRAYERS

The great prayer of thanksgiving and blessing, the Eucharistic Prayer, is "the center and high point of the entire celebration"[8] of the Eucharistic liturgy. Each of the Eucharistic Prayers approved for use in the Roman Rite and contained in *The Roman Missal* reflect the theme of reconciliation as we have discussed it thus far. The Eucharistic Prayer, in its very nature, is a prayer that both signifies and actualizes the reconciliation, or restoration of communion, between God and the world. Every Eucharistic Prayer is therefore a prayer of reconciliation. There is a particular focus, however, on the notion of reconciliation in two of the prayers of the Missal, fittingly known as Eucharistic Prayers for Reconciliation I and II.

These two prayers were original compositions and have their origin in Pope Paul VI's announcement of a Holy Year to be celebrated in 1975. In his public address calling for a Jubilee Year, Paul VI stated:

> The Holy Year has as its specific purpose a personal, inner, and therefore in some ways, outward renewal. The Holy Year is meant to be an available yet at the same time extraordinary form of therapy that must bring spiritual health to every conscience and, as a consequence, to social attitudes, at least to some degree. This is the general idea of the coming Holy Year and it is embodied in another central idea that is more particular and directed toward practice: the idea of reconciliation.
>
> The term "reconciliation" connotes as its opposite, separation. What sort of separation must we overcome in order to achieve the reconciliation that is the condition for the hoped-for renewal of the Jubilee? What kind of separation? Perhaps it is enough simply to state the three-word "reconciliation" in order to make us realize that our life is beset by too much separation, too much disharmony, too much disorder for us to be able to enjoy the gifts of individual and collective life as they are ideally meant to be.
>
> Before all else we are in need of reestablishing a genuine, vital and happy relationship with God, of being reconciled in humility and in love with him. From this first and constitutive harmony, the entire world of our experience can then be the expression of a need for reconciliation and can have its full impact in charity and justice to other persons in whom we will immediately acknowledge the right to be called our brothers and sisters. Reconciliation can then develop in other limitless and real spheres

---

8. *General Instruction of the Roman Missal* (GIRM), 78.

of existence: the community of the Church itself, society, politics, ecu-
menism, peace. If God permits us to celebrate the Holy Year, it will present many relevant ideas for us to elaborate.[9]

Reflecting the clearly stated Jubilee theme of reconciliation,
two new Eucharistic Prayers for Masses of Reconciliation, along with
three Eucharistic Prayers for Masses with Children, were approved by
the Sacred Congregation for Divine Worship in November 1974.[10]
The Eucharistic Prayers for Masses of Reconciliation were initially
approved as a three-year experiment and were not to be included in
official editions of *The Roman Missal*. With the third typical edition
of the Missal, however, the two Eucharistic Prayers for Reconciliation
are included and must now be considered as a stable part of the
euchology of the Roman Rite.

USE OF THE EUCHARISTIC PRAYERS FOR RECONCILIATION

As to the question of when and how these Eucharistic Prayers may be
used during the celebration of Mass, it is first important to note that
both Eucharistic Prayer for Reconciliation I (RI) and Eucharistic
Prayer for Reconciliation II (RII) have proper Prefaces which are
considered to be integral to the respective texts. This would seem,
at first glance, to greatly restrict the use of these Eucharistic Prayers
to days on the liturgical calendar without an obligatory proper preface
of their own. The relevant rubric, however, is as follows:

The Eucharistic Prayers for Reconciliation may be used in Masses
in which the mystery of reconciliation is conveyed to the faithful in
a special way, as for example, in the Masses For Promoting Harmony,
For Reconciliation, For the Preservation of Peace and Justice, In Time of
War or Civil Disturbance, For the Forgiveness of Sins, For Charity, of
the Mystery of the Holy Cross, of the Most Holy Eucharist, of the Most
Precious Blood of our Lord Jesus Christ, as well as in Masses during Lent.
Although these Eucharistic Prayers have been provided with a proper

---

9. Pope Paul VI, Address in St. Peter's, announcing the Holy Year 1975, May 9, 1973:
AAS 65 (1973), 322–325, in *Documents on the Liturgy: 1963–1979* (DOL), 4071.

10. Decree, *Postquam de Precibus*, November 1, 1974: Not 11 (1975) 4–6, in DOL,
1994–1998.

Preface, they may also be used with other Prefaces that refer to penance and conversion, as, for example, the Prefaces of Lent.[11]

These Eucharistic Prayers have long been considered especially suitable for use during Lent. These Forty Days are a privileged time of preparation for both catechumens and the faithful, through prayer, fasting, almsgiving, and other works of penance, to celebrate the Paschal Mystery with renewed and joyful hearts. *The Roman Missal* affirms the appropriateness of utilizing the Eucharistic Prayers for Reconciliation during Lent and makes clear that they should then be used in conjunction with one of the Prefaces for Lent. Thus, for example, if a priest celebrant were to choose to pray RI during the liturgy for the First Sunday of Lent, he should do so with the given Preface of the First Sunday of Lent, subtitled "The Temptation of the Lord."

We now turn to an exploration of the Eucharistic Prayers for Reconciliation individually. Given the fact, previously noted, that each Eucharistic Prayer has a proper Preface to be used under ordinary circumstances, the Prefaces will be examined as well.

EUCHARISTIC PRAYER FOR RECONCILIATION I

After the introductory dialogue between the priest and the assembly and an expression of thanks to the Father, who is called "holy," "almighty," and "eternal," the Preface for RI turns to the theme of life, specifically "the more abundant life" that is found through Jesus Christ. This reference evokes the words of Jesus in his discourse on the Good Shepherd: "I came that they may have life, and have it abundantly."[12] It is the life of grace, a life of friendship with the Lord, a communion of love that we come to possess as a result of God's invitation and the grace given to embrace it ("you never cease through her / to gather the whole human race into one"). Human beings are sinners in need of reconciliation, and the Father, "being rich in mercy," continues to invite us to approach him to receive pardon and forgiveness. The phrase *dives in misericordia* is derived from a beautiful passage from the Letter to the Ephesians, reflecting on God's plan of salvation:

11. *The Roman Missal.*
12. John 10:10.

But God, who is rich in mercy, because of the great love with which he loved us even when we were dead through our trespasses, made us alive together with Christ—by grace you have been saved—and raised us up with him and seated us with him in the heavenly places in Christ Jesus, so that in the ages to come he might show the immeasurable riches of his grace in kindness toward us in Christ Jesus.[13]

The richness of God's mercy and the gratuity of his gracious forgiveness is also reflective of one of the principal themes of the pontificate of John Paul II,[14] who canonized Saint Faustina Kowalska, the great apostle of Divine Mercy, and approved the decree by which the Second Sunday of Easter is now also known as the Sunday of the Divine Mercy.

The Preface next turns to the vitally important notion of "covenant." Covenant is at the very heart of the Judeo-Christian tradition and the reality that men and women "time and again have broken" this bond with God is clearly asserted. Although the idea of covenant is present in each of the Eucharistic Prayers of *The Roman Missal*, notably in the words of institution for the chalice ("the Blood of the new and eternal covenant"), RI perhaps more clearly reflects that the celebration of the Eucharist is the renewal and perfection of the covenant between God and humankind.[15] This perfection, indicated by the words "a new bond of love so tight / that it can never be undone" is linked with a particular ecclesiology, a vision of the Church as "family," gathered together as brothers and sisters in the Lord and children of the heavenly Father.

The next phrase expresses the truth that mercy and forgiveness are continually offered to us by God ("Even now you set before your people / a time of grace and reconciliation"), but also indicates the fitting use of this prayer during Lent. The call of God to repentance and the response of people through conversion is connected with the virtue of hope ("hope in Christ Jesus"). Recently, there has been a renewed emphasis on the necessity of hope in the Christian life, occasioned largely by the preaching and writing of Pope Benedict XVI,[16] whose apostolic visit to the United States of America in 2008

---

13. Ephesians 2:4–7, NRSV.

14. Cf. Pope John Paul II, *Dives in Misericordia* (1980).

15. Cf. *Sacrosanctum Concilium*, 10.

16. Cf. *Spe Salvi* (2007).

was carried out under the banner of "Christ our Hope." The celebration of the Eucharist and the reception of the sacrament of the Lord's Body and Blood feed our hope, they sustain us in our complete trust in God and his promises. As the theologian Paul McPartlan writes: "Christians are *sure* in their hope because they *experience* its fulfillment in anticipation every Sunday, when they do what the Lord commanded them to do in memory of him."[17]

The Preface for RI concludes with the people extolling the power of the Father's love and "proclaiming our joy / at the salvation that comes from you" as we prepare to sing the Sanctus. All of this is done as we are "filled with wonder." The language of wonder speaks of the child-like sense of awe with which we should be filled as we contemplate the holiness of the Trinity and celebrate the sacred mysteries of our salvation. John Paul II rightly referred to the "profound amazement and gratitude"[18] that should fill our hearts as we enter into the celebration of the eucharistic liturgy.

The body of RI commences with the statement that God, the "holy" one has been laboring from the very inception of the world "so that the human race may become holy, / just as you yourself are holy." Reconciliation, or restoration of communion, entails a transformation of men and women by God's grace. The universal call to perfect holiness given by God to all the faithful[19] begins in Baptism, but is sustained and perfected in the eucharistic sacrifice.

As the epiclesis upon the bread and wine begins, we are reminded that the offerings which will be "eucharistified," changed into the Eucharistic Body and Blood of the Lord, are "your people's offerings." Here is a powerful reminder of the goodness of creation and a foundational principle of Catholic sacramental-liturgical thought, namely that material elements, which come from God as Creator, are used as vehicles of the supernatural, as instruments of grace. The fact that the bread and wine are the gifts of the people and symbolic of the offering of their lives during the Mass is best expressed at the offertory

---

17. Paul McPartlan, *Sacrament of Salvation: An Introduction to Eucharistic Ecclesiology,* London: T&T Clark Ltd., 1995, page 5.

18. *Ecclesia de Eucharistia,* 5.

19. Cf. *Lumen Gentium,* 11.

when members of the faithful present the elements that will become our spiritual food and drink.[20]

After the priest makes the Sign of the Cross over the bread and chalice, it is stated that in Jesus Christ "we, too, are your sons and daughters." The prayer does not speak of becoming sons and daughters of the Father, but reflects the truth that we are already the children of God by virtue of our Baptism. Once again, the language of sons and daughters reflects the image of the Church as the family of God, united around the family banquet of the Eucharist.

The beginning of the Institution narrative of RI ("though we once were lost") once again evokes the image of a loving Father who is persistent in seeking out and reconciling men and women created in his image. God the Father is not only willing to forgive and heal his children, but is active in pursuing us when we go astray.[21] The Eucharistic Prayer continues with an emphasis that Jesus was obedient to the mission given him by the Father and freely embraced his suffering and Death on the Cross for one motive: out of love ("for our sake"). After a return to the notion of covenant and its explicit connection with the Cross ("lasting sign of your covenant"), the Institution narrative asserts "he desired to celebrate the Passover with his disciples." Notwithstanding the sometimes vigorous debates among exegetes regarding the discrepancy between the chronology of the Synoptic accounts of the Gospel and John's account with respect to the timing of the Last Supper, there can be no question that the celebration of the Eucharist, rooted in the historical words and actions of Jesus at his final meal with his disciples, is inextricably linked with the Passover and the passage from slavery to freedom, from light to darkness, from death to the fullness of life. The risen Christ is the fulfillment of the Law and the prophets: he is the New Covenant, he is the new Exodus, he is the new Passover.[22]

Echoing the great Christological hymn from the Letter to the Colossians, the words of Institution pertaining to the chalice make clear that it is in the person of Christ himself, particularly through the shedding of his blood on the Cross, that reconciliation is definitively

---

20. Cf. *General Instruction of the Roman Missal*, 73.

21. Cf. Luke 15. The parables of the Lost Sheep, the Lost Coin, and the Prodigal Son exemplify this image of the Father.

22. Cf. 1 Corinthians 5:6–8.

accomplished. Furthermore, it is clear that this reconciliation involves not only humankind, but indeed all of creation ("he was about to reconcile all things in himself").[23] This reflects the vision put forth in both the Pauline and Johannine biblical testimony that speaks of the transformation and renewal of the entire world through the risen Lord.[24]

Following the Mystery of Faith, the anamnesis portion of RI returns to the previous themes of Christ as "our Passover" and "the Victim who reconciles mankind" to the Father. In the midst of this passage, we also find a beautiful phrase referring to Christ as "our surest peace." Peace, of course, is earnestly sought in many corners of the world where there has been and continues to be much strife and bloodshed. The prayer reminds us that true and lasting peace is the fruit of reconciliation with God through Christ, which then empowers the transformation of human relationships, both at the interpersonal level as well as between nations and cultures.

The second moment of epiclesis, in which the priest prays that the fruits of the sacrifice unite the assembly gathered for the celebration, makes explicit reference to the Church as a Body. The ecclesiology rooted in the image of the Church as the Body of Christ, found throughout the New Testament writings of Paul and in the Fathers of the Church, was happily revived in the last century, largely through the efforts of Pope Pius XII,[25] who also affirmed the positive contributions of the liturgical movement and furthered the cause of liturgical reform. The understanding of the Church in dynamic, biblical, patristic, and liturgical images such as body of Christ and family of God serve as an effective antidote to a sometimes exaggerated emphasis on the Church as an juridical organization or a hierarchical pyramid.

The intercessory section of RI provides us with another significant ecclesiological concept. The priest prays that we may be kept always "in communion of mind and heart" with the Pope and the diocesan Bishop. Communion is "the central and fundamental idea"[26] in the theology of the Church presented in the documents of Vatican II. We pray for the Bishop of Rome and the local Bishop in each celebration of the Mass, reflecting the particular assembly's union with the

---

23. Colossians 1:15–20.

24. Cf. Revelation 21:5; Romans 8:18–23.

25. Cf. Pope Pius XII, *Mystici Corporis* (1943) and *Mediator Dei* (1947).

26. World Synod of Bishops, Final Report of the 1985 Extraordinary Synod.

broader Church. Reconciliation with God always occurs in conjunction with reconciliation with the community of believers. Our unity with the Pope and his brother bishops is much more than something legalistic. The Church is not a club and the Christian faith is not a hobby. Rather, the Church is a communion in faith, hope, and love, united with and under our Head, Jesus Christ. This communion is manifested above all in the celebration of the Eucharist. From the very first days of the Church, worship in the form of the liturgical action of the Lord's Supper went hand in hand with the witness of the apostles: "They devoted themselves to the apostles' teaching and fellowship, to the breaking of bread and the prayers."[27] This unity in both apostolic faith and liturgical praxis, indicated by the venerable maxim *lex orandi, lex credendi*, continues to be lived and celebrated in the Church of the twenty-first century.

RI continues with an eschatological perspective that looks ahead toward final judgment and the fullness of life in the Kingdom of Heaven, along with a sense that the Church includes those who have gone before. We pray that we may one day stand before the Father "saints among saints, in the halls of heaven, / with the Blessed Virgin Mary, Mother of God, / the blessed Apostles and all the Saints, / and with our deceased brothers and sisters." In the celebration of the liturgy on earth, we experience a foretaste and participate here and now in the wedding feast of the Lamb, united with the holy men and women who have preceded us.

The Eucharistic Prayer, prior to the final doxology, concludes with a synthesis of salvation history, as we are "freed at last from the wound of corruption," referring to original sin and the fall of our first parents, and "made fully into a new creation," looking ahead to our final destination in the glory of God's Kingdom. As we were spiritually reborn and made a new creation through the Sacrament of Baptism, this newness is brought to perfection when we gaze upon the face of God and share in the communion of Trinitarian love.

EUCHARISTIC PRAYER FOR RECONCILIATION II

The expression of thanksgiving at the beginning of the Preface for Eucharistic Prayer II praises God the almighty Father "for all you do

---

27. Acts 2:42, NRSV.

in this world." The Father is recognized as Creator, the one who is the source of all that has been, all that is, and all that ever will be. The creative activity of God that brought the world into existence also sustains it in being. Yet the motive for thanks and praise is not limited simply to God as the author of life, but also as the one who saves his people and reconciles them to himself.

The Preface continues with a statement about fallen humanity and the disunity and alienation that has occurred as a result of sin. In asserting that "the human race / is divided by dissension and discord," RII recognizes that sin not only ruptures our communion with God but our relationships with each other. The human family now suffers from a lack of harmony within itself, as men and women see each other as obstacles to be overcome or opponents to be defeated, rather than brothers and sisters to be loved. This is reflected in the very first pages of the Bible, in the story of our earliest ancestors. After Adam's sin, his response to God is to deflect the blame onto Eve,[28] the one who has been given as his suitable partner, bone of his bones and flesh of his flesh. The narrative regarding humanity given in Genesis continues with the account of Cain, who attacks and kills his brother Abel out of resentment and jealousy.[29] Envy, rivalry, violence, and a lack of respect for others endure in our world to this day.

Nevertheless, the Preface proceeds on a note of hope, derived from the reality that "you change our hearts / to prepare them for reconciliation." It is the grace of God that touches the hearts of men and women and leads them toward the healing of their relationships and the restoration of communion. True change, the authentic transformation known as *metanoia*, has its origin in the God of mercy and reconciliation. RII also states that human beings know this "from experience." This speaks to the fact that God is present and active in our lives and each of us, though wounded by sin, possesses the capacity to recognize God and his works. The theme of God's grace moving us toward reconciliation is developed as the Preface continues, with an emphasis on the role of the Holy Spirit: "by your Spirit you move human hearts." The third person of the Trinity, consubstantial with the Father and the Son and inseparable from them, "is also the Consoler

---

28. Cf. Genesis 3:12.
29. Cf. Genesis 4:1–8.

who gives the human heart grace for repentance and conversion."[30]
The tangible results of this grace at work in our lives are expressed in
vivid, beautiful terms, which call us to overcome our tendency toward
cynicism and resignation: "enemies may speak to each other again, /
adversaries may join hands, / and peoples seek to meet together."
RII continues in this vein, noting that God's power causes hatred to
be overcome by love, revenge to give way to forgiveness, and discord
to be changed to mutual respect.

Following the Sanctus, RII begins with a series of three
powerful Christological images. Jesus Christ is first referred to as "the
Word that brings salvation," evoking the prologue of John's account
of the Gospel[31] and leading us to meditate on the mystery of the
Incarnation, God-with-us. The Son of God is also "the hand you extend
to sinners." Although there is no explicit reference in the Scriptures to
Christ as "the hand of the Father," the New Testament frequently
depicts Jesus reaching out to others, touching those in need, extending
his hands toward those in need of healing, both physically and
spiritually. This gesture, communicating both intimacy and authority,
is reflected in the Church's sacraments of healing, as the priest lays his
hands on the head of a seriously ill person in the celebration of the
Anointing of the Sick or extends his hands above the head of a penitent
when pronouncing the words of absolution during the Rite of Penance.

Finally, Jesus is called "the way by which your peace is offered
to us." We are reminded of Jesus' words to Thomas at the beginning
of his discourse at the Last Supper: "I am the way, and the truth, and
the life. No one comes to the Father except through me."[32] Jesus is not
one path among many, but he, and he alone, is the way that leads to
true peace, the *shalom* of communion with God and one another.

RII makes clear that, having repented of our sins and thus
being reconciled to God, "we might love another / through your
Son." Love, of course, is a word that we hear and use frequently.
Unfortunately, love is often used in frivolous or casual manner, in
circumstances where the words "like," "prefer," or "enjoy" might be
more suitable. Jesus told his friends gathered on the evening before he
died: "This is my commandment, that you love one another as I have

---

30. CCC, 1433; cf. John 15:26; Acts 2:36–38.

31. Cf. John 1:1–5, 14.

32. John 14:6.

loved you. No one has greater love than this, to lay down one's life for one's friends."[33] True love, authentic charity, is rooted in God's love and entails the gift of self, the willingness to sacrifice for the good of the other. This sacrificial love is celebrated and manifested every time we gather for the Eucharist.

Furthermore, Jesus Christ is the one "whom for our sake you handed over to death." This phrase, filled with theological importance, is apt to be misunderstood by those who view the Passion and Death of the Lord as the price exacted by an angry and vengeful God as the cost of our reconciliation. There are two related truths that are communicated in this statement. First of all, the Death of Jesus is indeed for us; secondly, God's love for his people is so vast, indeed boundless, that he allowed even his only Son to give his life for us. The Church proclaims: "By giving up his own Son for our sins, God manifests that his plan for us is one of benevolent love, prior to any merit on our part."[34]

As the epiclesis over the gifts begins, RII uses language that emphasizes the "today-ness" of the liturgical celebration: "And now, / celebrating the reconciliation / Christ has brought us, / we entreat you . . ." Through the action of the risen Lord and the power of the Holy Spirit, the offering of the Eucharist here and now represents the Paschal Mystery of our redemption and also anticipates the glorious feast of the Kingdom of Heaven. The Eucharistic celebration, in a unique and mysterious way, unites the historical past and the eschatological future in the liturgical present.

The introduction to the words of Institution for the bread provides us with yet another way of understanding our reconciliation in and through Christ: "when about to give his life to set us free." Freedom, like love, is another word subject to misuse and misunderstanding in contemporary culture. RII here refers first of all to the liberation from sin and death that we have received through the death and Resurrection of the Lord. Having been set free, however, does not imply that we now possess absolute autonomy, an ability to choose that is unrestricted and unfettered. Saint Paul wrote to the community at Corinth: "Do you not know that your body is a temple of the Holy

33. John 15:12–13.
34. CCC, 604.

Spirit within you, which you have from God, and that you are not your own? For you were bought with a price; therefore glorify God in your body."[35] The gift of reconciliation we have received comes with a responsibility, a call to be holy as Christ is holy. As the *Catechism of the Catholic Church* teaches:

> Freedom is the power, rooted in reason and will, to act or not to act, to do this or that, and so to perform deliberate actions on one's own responsibility. By free will one shapes one's own life. Human freedom is a force for growth and maturity in truth and goodness; it attains its perfection when directed toward God, our beatitude.

> The more one does what is good, the freer one becomes. There is no true freedom except in the service of what is good and just.[36]

Transitioning to the words of Institution over the chalice, the priest says: "he took the chalice of blessing in his hands, / confessing your mercy." The language utilized here is significant on two levels. First of all, the "chalice of blessing" provides an explicit link not only to the teaching of Paul,[37] but also to the third cup consumed at the Seder meal of Passover. Secondly, the mercy of God is proclaimed not primarily in the words of Jesus, but above all through that which is signified by handing over the cup to his disciples, namely his blood that will be shed on the Cross of Calvary.

The anamnesis section of RII clearly associates our reconciliation with memorial and sacrifice. Memorial, the preferred translation in English of the Greek *anamnesis*, is much more than a mere commemoration or remembrance of a past event. Rather, the liturgical action, celebrated though sacramental signs and symbols, makes the memorialized event real and present for us today so that we may participate in it. In the Mass, therefore, we continue to enter into the death and Resurrection of the Lord. The notion of memorial with regard to the Eucharist is intrinsically related to that of sacrifice. Again, the *Catechism* states: "The Eucharist is the memorial of Christ's Passover, the making present and the sacramental offering of his unique sacrifice, in the liturgy of the Church which is his Body."[38] It is

---

35. 1 Corinthians 6:19–20.
36. CCC, 1731, 1733.
37. Cf. 1 Corinthians 10:16.
38. CCC, 1362.

through our participation in the sacrifice of Christ that reconciliation truly occurs.

In the communion epiclesis, the invocation of the gifts of the Spirit upon the congregation, the Eucharistic celebration is referred to as "this saving banquet." The Mass is truly a sacred meal in which Christ offers himself as our spiritual food and drink. Jesus himself instructs us: "Very truly, I tell you, unless you eat the flesh of the Son of Man and drink his blood, you have no life in you."[39] Participation in the banquet of Christ's Body and Blood frees us from our venial sins and strengthens us to live out our baptismal promises.

The intercessions of RII pray that God may make the Church "a sign of unity / and an instrument of peace among all people." As Christ is the sacrament of God the Father, so the Church is the sacrament of Christ to the world. In other words, the Church is the sign and instrument of communion between God and the world, and among the members of the human family.[40] The Church preaches peace and reconciliation, and labors that all people may be gathered together in fellowship. These labors embrace all aspects of the Church's activity, from the Holy Father's annual address on January 1, the World Day of Peace, to the Holy See's engagement in attempting to settle regional conflicts. They embrace the efforts of an urban parish to rid their streets of drugs, guns, and gang violence, to the establishment of Church-run clinics to care for children orphaned as a result of civil wars. Above all, the Church labors for peace through her constant prayer and the celebration of the Eucharist in particular.

As is the case with RI, RII prays that all the members of the Body of Christ may be preserved in communion the Pope and the diocesan Bishop. The priest prays that, as we are gathered together at the table of the Lord, we may one day be gathered with the Blessed Virgin, the Apostles, and all the Saints who have preceded us, "and those of every race and tongue / who have died in your friendship." This clearly speaks of God's universal salvific will and the universality of the Church. All people, regardless of their ethnic background, the color of their skin, their socio-economic background, or any other factor of distinction, are invited to know the Lord Jesus Christ and to be reconciled with the Father through him. This eternal gathering in the Kingdom is "the unending banquet of unity / in a new heaven and a new earth," echoing the words of the book of Revelation and its vision of the New Jerusalem.[41]

CONCLUSION

For many centuries, the Roman Canon was the exclusive Eucharistic Prayer of the Roman Rite. With the liturgical reforms ushered as a result of the Second Vatican Council, the Church has moved toward great diversity in its euchology, providing several additional anaphoras intended to contribute to the liturgical celebration at different times and under different circumstances. The two Eucharistic Prayers for Reconciliation are valuable additions to the Church's treasury of worship prayers. While sharing the same core elements (thanksgiving, epiclesis, words of Institution, anamnesis and offering, intercessions, and final doxology / great Amen) as the other Eucharistic Prayers in *The Roman Missal*, RI and RII provide us with the opportunity to focus on the theme of reconciliation, at times when it should be front and center in the hearts and minds of the members of the community. These occasions may be predictable, as in the case of the season of Lent, or they may come upon us suddenly and without warning, as when war breaks out among nations or a terrorist attack occurs.

Each of us has been called to give witness to Jesus Christ in every dimension of our lives. Having been reconciled with God through Baptism and seeking to intensify our communion with him, especially through the sacrament of the Eucharist, we must then be true apostles of reconciliation in our families, our places of work, our neighborhoods and our culture at large. In a world still scarred by brokenness and disillusionment, by deep-seated hatreds and stunning acts of violence, the possibility, indeed the necessity, of reconciliation with God and with each other must be preached, celebrated, and lived by every Christian person. Saint Francis of Assisi famously prayed that God might make him an instrument of peace. As the Church of today prays the anaphoras of Reconciliation, may our fervent prayer be "Lord, make us instruments of your reconciliation!"

---

41. Revelation 2:1; see also Isaiah 65:17.

Chapter 7

The Eucharistic Prayers for Various Needs and Occasions

Monsignor James P. Moroney, STB, STL

A BRIEF HISTORY

Originally prepared in German by the Swiss Synod as an alternative Eucharistic Prayer, the *Prex eucharistica quæ in Missis pro variis necessitatibus adhiberi potest* was approved by the Sacred Congregation for Divine Worship in August of 1974. The prayer was subsequently translated into the other two languages used in Switzerland (French and Italian).

In response to an increasing desire for additional Eucharistic Prayers, the text was approved over the next thirteen years for use in 12 languages, including the Spanish language *texto unico* in 1989. Thus the prayer was first introduced to the dioceses of the United States in the Spanish language.

On August 6, 1991,[1] the Congregation for Divine Worship and the Discipline of the Sacraments published a revised Latin version of the Swiss Synod Eucharistic Prayer under the title: *Eucharistic Prayer for Masses for Various Needs and Occasions*, noting that "Since from the very beginning different editions of the text of this eucharistic prayer have been available in German, French, and Italian, it seems necessary to issue a Latin text of this prayer to serve as the *editio typica* for all languages." The new text was definitive for all subsequent editions.

In that same decree, the Congregation commented on the nature of the Eucharistic Prayer as "the summit of the entire celebration of the Mass," whose purpose is that "the entire congregation joins

---

1. Prot. CD 511/91.

itself to Christ in acknowledging the great things God has done in offering the paschal sacrifice."[2]

The decree continues by noting the particular and changeable role of the intercessions, expressed in various formulas in the various Eucharistic Prayers of *The Roman Missal*, particularly in regard to Ritual Masses.[3]

Thus does the publication and use of the Eucharistic Prayer for Various Needs and Occasions likewise provide variable intercessions and Prefaces appropriate to Masses from the section of the Missal bearing the same name.

In November of 1994, the National Conference of Catholic Bishops approved an interim English language edition of the prayers which had been prepared by the International Commission on English in the Liturgy. The prayers were confirmed by the Holy See on May 9, 1995,[4] and was published as a separate fascicle. In an August 15, 1995, decree, signed by Cardinal William Keeler, then NCCB President, the prayers were provided for publication and used as of October 1, 1995.

---

2. Ibid.

3. In addition to the various proper prefaces for the Ritual Masses, several other proper texts are provided for the Eucharistic Prayers:

For the Conferral of Baptism and the Mass for the Scrutinies the proper forms of the *Memento, Domine* and the *Hanc Igitur* are given, with proper intercessions for Eucharistic Prayers II and III.

In the Ordination of a Bishop, Priests, or Deacons the newly ordained is prayed for in proper formulas for the *Hanc Igitur* and in proper intercessions for Eucharistic Prayers II, III, and IV.

For the Consecration of Virgins, a proper formula for the *Hanc Igitur* and proper intercessions for Eucharistic Prayers II, III, and IV are provided.

For the Conferral of Confirmation, for the Blessing of an Abbot or Abbess, and when the Celebration of Marriage takes place during Mass, a proper form of the *Hanc Igitur* is given, with proper intercessions for Eucharistic Prayers II and III.

While here are no changeable parts of the Eucharistic Prayer for the Mass of First Religious Profession or the Mass for the Renewal of Vows, in the Mass of Final Profession "the oblation of the professed is appropriately commemorated" with a proper *Hanc Igitur*, and proper intercessions in Eucharistic Prayers II, III, and IV.

Because only the Roman Canon or Eucharistic Prayer III are used for the Dedication of a Church and an Altar, a proper form of the *Hanc Igitur* and Proper Intercessions for Eucharistic Prayer III are provided.

No changeable parts are provided for the Eucharistic Prayers for The Institution of Lectors and Acolytes.

4. Prot N 92/95/L.

THE TEXT

The Eucharistic Prayers for Various Needs and Occasions are really one prayer with four sets of Prefaces and intercessions based on four themes:

- The Church on the Path of Unity[5]
- God Guides His Church along the Way of Salvation[6]
- Jesus, the Way to the Father[7]
- Jesus, Who Went About Doing Good[8]

Since the 1991 edition of the Holy See, this has been rendered as four separate Eucharistic Prayers, although all but the Prefaces and intercessions remain the same for each of the prayers.

The prayer, as the title indicates, is to be used for Masses for Various Needs and Occasions. Each prayer must be used with its own Preface which, like Eucharistic Prayer IV, is integral to the text.

Each of these Eucharistic Prayers are preceded by a rubric that notes which Mass sets from the Eucharistic Prayers for Various Needs and Occasions would most appropriately indicate their use.

Eucharistic Prayer	Appropriate Mass Sets
I. The Church on the Path of Unity	For the Church
	For the Pope
	For the Bishop
	For the Election of a Pope or a Bishop
	For a Council or Synod
	For Priest
	For the Priest Himself
	For Ministers of the Church,
	For a Spiritual or Pastoral Gathering
II. God Guides His Church along the Way of Salvation	For the Church
	For Vocations to Holy Orders
	For the Laity
	For the Family
	For Religious
	For Vocations to Religious Life
	For Charity
	For Relatives and Friends
	For Giving Thanks to God

---

5. Previously rendered *The Church on the Way to Unity*.

6. Previously rendered *God Guides the Church on the Way of Salvation*.

7. Previously rendered *Jesus, Way to the Father*.

8. Previously rendered *Jesus, the Compassion of God*.

Eucharistic Prayer	*Appropriate Mass Sets*
III. Jesus, the Way to the Father	For the Evangelization of Peoples
	For Persecuted Christians
	For the Nation or State
	For Those in Public Office
	For a Governing Assembly
	At the Beginning of the Civil Year
	For the Progress of Peoples
IV. Jesus, Who Went About Doing Good	For Refugees and Exiles
	In Time of Famine or For Those Suffering Hunger
	For Our Oppressors
	For Those Held in Captivity
	For Those in Prison
	For the Sick
	For the Dying
	For the Grace of a Happy Death
	In Any Need

The Common Parts of the Four Eucharistic Prayers for Various Needs

The Preface

The Preface is changeable; please see page 88.

Post-Sanctus Thanksgiving[9]

The Post-Sanctus thanksgiving begins, like all the Eucharistic Prayers, echoing the holiness of God in the preceding Sanctus. Establishing a particularly contemporary tone from the outset, the prayer addresses God as the one who loves us and walks with us on the journey of life. The Son is the blessed one in our midst, equally echoing the Sanctus: "blessed is he who comes in the name of the Lord."

---

9. "You are indeed Holy and to be glorified, O God, / who love the human race, / and who always walk with us on the journey of life. / Blessed indeed is your Son, / present in our midst / when we are gathered by his love, / and when, as once for the disciples, so now for us, / he opens the Scriptures and breaks the bread."

Epiclesis[10]

The Epiclesis is brief and straight-forward, asking that the Father send forth the Holy Spirit so that the gifts of bread and wine "may become for us the Body and Blood of our Lord, Jesus Christ."

Consecration and Memorial Acclamation

Please see page 79.

Memorial[11]

A unique and contemporary reflection on the relationship of the Father and the Son begins the Memorial as the Son is described as him "whom you led through his Passion and Death on the Cross to the glory of the Resurrection, / and whom you have seated at your right hand," paralleling the proclamation that "we proclaim the work of your love until he comes again and we offer you the Bread of life / and the Chalice of blessing."

The memorial continues by asking God to look favorably upon the Church's oblation, showing forth the Paschal sacrifice "that has been handed on to us" and by the Spirit of his love to count us now and "until the day of eternity" among the members of Christ, in whose Body and Blood we have communion.

The First Intercession

This is changeable. Please see the following.

---

10. "Therefore, Father most merciful, / we ask that you send forth your Holy Spirit / to sanctify these gifts of bread and wine, / that they may become for us / the Body and + Blood / of our Lord, Jesus Christ."

11. "Therefore, holy Father, / as we celebrate the memorial of Christ your Son, our Savior, / whom you led through his Passion and Death on the Cross / to the glory of the Resurrection, / and whom you have seated at your right hand, / we proclaim the work of your love until he comes again / and we offer you the Bread of life / and the Chalice of blessing.

Look with favor on the oblation of your Church, / in which we show forth / the paschal Sacrifice of Christ that has been handed on to us, / and grant that, / by the power of the Spirit of your love, / we may be counted now and until the day of eternity / among the members of your Son, / in whose Body and Blood we have communion."

Two Unchangeable Intercessions

The first of the unchangeable intercessions is for the dead in two groups: our brothers and sisters who sleep in the peace of Christ and all the dead whose faith is known only to God. God is asked to admit them to rejoice in the light of his face and to give them fullness of life through the Resurrection.

The second intercession is for ourselves, that we might come to live with God forever in communion with the Virgin Mary and all the saints in exaltation and praise through Christ.

The Changeable Parts of the Four Eucharistic Prayers for Various Needs

1. The Church on the Path of Unity

Summary of the Changeable Preface and Intercession[12]
The Preface proclaims that in the Gospel of his Son, God has brought together one Church from many peoples, filled with life by the power of his Spirit, as he gathers the whole human race into one. The Church brings about this unity by manifesting the covenant of love, eternally dispensing the blessed hope of the Kingdom through Christ Jesus.

Thus do we ask that through a renewal of the Church, the bond of unity of faithful pastors, Pope, bishops, the Order of Bishops and the clergy, that "in a world torn by strife your people may shine forth as a prophetic sign of unity and concord."

Development of this Theme in the Collects
This theme is further developed in Collects of the recommended Masses for Various Needs. From all the nations, God never ceases to gather to himself, in the covenant of his Christ, "a people growing

---

12. **Preface:** "For by the word of your Son's Gospel / you have brought together one Church / from every people, tongue, and nation, / and, having filled her with life by the power of your Spirit, / you never cease through her / to gather the whole human race into one.

Manifesting the covenant of your love, / she dispenses without ceasing / the blessed hope of your Kingdom / and shines bright as the sign of your faithfulness, / which in Christ Jesus our Lord you promised would last for eternity."

Intercessions: "Lord, renew your Church (which is in N.) / by the light of the Gospel. / Strengthen the bond of unity / between the faithful and the pastors of your people, / together with N. our Pope, N. our Bishop, / and the whole Order of Bishops, / that in a world torn by strife / your people may shine forth / as a prophetic sign of unity and concord."

together in unity through the Spirit." This people is assembled from all nations.[13]

The Collects pray that the Church "always remain that holy people, / formed as one by the unity of Father, Son and Holy Spirit, which manifests to the world the Sacrament of your holiness and unity and leads it to the perfection of your charity."[14] Just as Christ has revealed the Father's glory to all nations, so the holy Church perseveres with steadfast faith in confessing God's name throughout the world,[15] becoming "a sign and instrument in the world of the presence of Christ."[16]

Thus do we pray that the Pope be "a visible source and foundation / of unity in faith and of communion,"[17] that the Bishop may through his governance "build up in the world the sacrament of the Church,"[18] that priests have "a persevering obedience" to God's will,[19] and that all the faithful "in truth and charity" be made one people through "abundance of grace, mercy and peace."[20]

2. God Guides His Church along the Way of Salvation

Summary of the Changeable Preface and Intercession[21]
God the Creator is ever at work in his creation, guiding his Church on her pilgrim journey today, just as he guided the chosen people through the desert. By the power of the Holy Spirit, he leads her along the paths of time to the eternal joy of his kingdom.

---

13. For the Church, Collect B.

14. For the Church, Collect C.

15. Cf. For the Church, Collect D

16. For the Church, Collect E

17. For the Pope, First Collect.

18. For the Bishop, Third Collect.

19. For Priests, Second Collect .

20. For a Spiritual or Pastoral Gathering, Second Collect.

21. **Preface:** "For you never forsake the works of your wisdom, / but by your providence are even now at work in our midst. / With mighty hand and outstretched arm / you led your people Israel through the desert. / Now, as your Church makes her pilgrim journey in the world, / you always accompany her / by the power of the Holy Spirit, / and lead her along the paths of time / to the eternal joy of your Kingdom, / through Christ our Lord."

Intercessions: "And so, having called us to your table, Lord, / confirm us in unity, / so that, together with N. our Pope and N. our Bishop, / with all Bishops, Priests and Deacons, / and your entire people, / as we walk your ways with faith and hope, we may strive to bring joy and trust into the world."

Thus do we ask the one who has called us to his table to confirm us in unity with the Pope, the Bishop, the priests, the deacons, and all his people as we walk his ways with faith and hope. May we strive to bring joy and trust into the world.

Development of this Theme in the Collects

God the Creator is ever at work in his creation and never ceases to gather to himself a people from all nations, to grow together in unity through the Spirit.[22] He raises up worthy ministers for his altars and makes them ardent yet gentle heralds of his Gospel.[23] God makes the lay faithful "fervent with the Christian spirit" that they might constantly build up the Kingdom in this world,[24] and establishes in family life a firm foundation, that through "the bonds of charity"[25] we might one day delight in the eternal rewards of the Father's house.[26]

3. Jesus, the Way to the Father

Summary of the Changeable Preface and Intercession [27]

The Word through whom the world was made is given to us by the Mediator who teaches us the way to God, the truth that sets us free, and the life that fills us with gladness through Christ. The Father gathers us into a family, redeemed by the Blood of his Cross and signed with the seal of the Spirit.

---

22. Cf. For the Church, Collect C.

23. For Vocations to Holy Orders, Collect.

24. Cf. For Vocations to Holy Orders, Collect.

25. For the Family, Collect.

26. Cf. For the Family, Collect.

27. **Preface**: "For by your Word you created the world / and you govern all things in harmony. / You gave us the same Word made flesh as Mediator, / and he has spoken your words to us/ and called us to follow him. / He is the way that leads us to you, / the truth that sets us free, / the life that fills us with gladness. / Through your Son you gather men and women, / whom you made for the glory of your name, / into one family, / redeemed by the Blood of his Cross / and signed with the seal of the Spirit."

Intercessions: "By our partaking of this mystery, almighty Father, / give us life through your Spirit, / grant that we may be conformed to the image of your Son, / and confirm us in the bond of communion, / together with N. our Pope and N. our Bishop, / with all other Bishops, / with Priests and Deacons, / and with your entire people. / Grant that all the faithful of the Church, / looking into the signs of the times by the light of faith, / may constantly devote themselves / to the service of the Gospel. / Keep us attentive to the needs of all / that, sharing their grief and pain, / their joy and hope, / we may faithfully bring them the good news of salvation / and go forward with them / along the way of your Kingdom."

Thus do we ask that by our partaking of the Eucharist, we might receive life, be conformed to the image of Christ, and be made one with the Pope, the Bishop, the clergy, and the faithful. Two additional petitions follow: that by the light of faith, we might read the signs of the times and serve the Gospel and that God might keep us attentive to those in need, that we might bring them the Good News and go forward with them along the way to God's Kingdom.

Development of this Theme in the Collects

Through the Son of God, the world's true light,[28] God has established his Church as "the sacrament of salvation for all nations,"[29] working for the salvation of every creature and ever seeking to lead the all the peoples on earth into "one family and one people" of God.[30] "Sustained by the power of the Sacraments," God's people "advance in the path of salvation and love,"[31] ever seeking to be united to the sufferings of Christ, as faithful witnesses to his promise.[32]

This witness carries the Gospel to the world, ever seeking the "prosperity of peoples, / the assurance of peace, / and freedom of religion"[33] in order that God might gather one family to himself, fill all hearts with the fire of his love, and kindle in them a love of neighbor so that every division might be removed and "each human person may be brought to perfection."[34]

4. Jesus, Who Went about Doing Good

Summary of the Changeable Preface and Intercession[35]

God has given us his Son as our Lord and Redeemer, who cared for the children, the poor, sinners, the oppressed, and the afflicted.

---

28. Cf. For Evangelization of Peoples, Collect A-1.

29. For Evangelization of Peoples, Collect B.

30. For Evangelization of Peoples, Collect B.

31. For the Evangelization of Peoples, Collect.

32. For Persecuted Christians, Collect.

33. For Those in Public Office, Collect.

34. For the Progress of Peoples, Collect.

35. **Preface:** "For you have given us Jesus Christ, your Son, / as our Lord and Redeemer. / He always showed compassion / for children and for the poor, / for the sick and for sinners, / and he became a neighbor / to the oppressed and the afflicted. / By word and deed he announced to the world / that you are our Father / and that you care for all your sons and daughters."

Intercessions: "Bring your Church, O Lord, / to perfect faith and charity, / together with N. our Pope and N. our Bishop, / with all Bishops, Priests and Deacons, / and the entire

Thus, by word and deed, did he make known God's care for his sons and daughters.

Thus, do we ask God to bring us to perfect faith and charity with the Pope, our Bishop, the clergy, and the people, to help us to see and comfort those who labor and are burdened, serving them after the example of Christ. Thus, may the Church stand as a living witness to truth and freedom, to peace and justice, so that all people may be raised up to a new hope.

Development of this Theme in the Collects

No one is a stranger to the Lord and no one is ever distant from his help.[36] He "look[s] with compassion on refugees and exiles, / on segregated persons and on lost children";[37] thus, does the Church pray to the God who provides for all creatures, that he grant us an effective love so "that famine may be banished / and that they may have strength to serve you / with free and untroubled hearts."[38] We beg God to "drive out, in your compassion, / the hunger of your servants;"[39] sincerely love all who afflict us, return only good for evil;[40] redeem all captives from sin;[41] give knowledge to the sick that they are blessed;[42] and give the dying the grace to "leave this world without stain of sin."[43]

CONCLUSION

The Eucharistic Prayers for Various Needs and Occasions present us with a form of Eucharistic Prayer that is unique in the history of the Roman Rite. By use of a series of thematic Prefaces and intercessions

---

people you have made your own. / Open our eyes to the needs of our brothers and sisters; / inspire in us words and actions to comfort those who labor and are burdened. / Make us serve them truly, / after the example of Christ and at his command. / And may your Church stand as a living witness / to truth and freedom, / to peace and justice, / that all people may be raised up to a new hope."

36. Cf. For Refugees and Exiles, Collect.
37. For Refugees and Exiles, Collect.
38. In Time of Famine or for Those Suffering From Hunger, Collect A.
39. In Time of Famine or for Those Suffering From Hunger, Collect B.
40. Cf. For Our Oppressors, Collect.
41. Cf. For Those Held in Captivity, Collect.
42. For the Sick, Collect.
43. For the Grace of a Happy Death, Collect.

intended to address contemporary needs and occasions, the prayer can play a limited but important role in the liturgical life of the Church.

While the pastoral utility of these prayers and their place in the organic growth of the Mass of the Roman Rite is a work in progress, their presence in the third edition of *The Roman Missal* provides yet another tool for pastors of souls to seek God's gracious assistance in addressing a wide range of particular religious and secular needs.

Chapter 8

Initiation Texts in
The Roman Missal

Reverend Ronald J. Lewinski, STL

The revised edition of *The Roman Missal* provides the opportunity
to review the liturgical texts relative to the Sacraments of Christian
Initiation. For many pastoral ministers, liturgists, and catechists, the
Rite of Christian Initiation of Adults (RCIA) may be the only source
that is thought of when it comes to prayer texts for the initiation
sacraments. *The Roman Missal*, however, contains a host of texts that
are often overlooked. Among these are the Mass texts for the Rite
of Election, the three Lenten Scrutinies, and the celebration of
Baptism at Mass outside of the Easter Vigil. In addition to these texts
we find the inclusion in the Missal of the entire Easter Vigil, Mass
texts for Confirmation liturgies, and orations for Votive Masses of the
Most Holy Eucharist, which may be used for First Holy Communion
celebrations. Preparing to celebrate the rites of Christian Initiation
requires a study of both the revised Missal and the RCIA side by side.

Under the principle of *lex orandi, lex credendi* (the law of prayer
is the law of belief), it is the full complement of all these prayer texts
that gives us a fuller picture of the Church's spirituality of Christian
initiation.

We will look at how and when these initiation texts are used
pastorally and how the new translation of these texts in the third
edition of *The Roman Missal* might enrich our appreciation for the
theology and spirituality of Christian Initiation that we find imbedded
in the texts.

The Election or Enrollment of Names

While the Rite of Reception into the Order of Catechumens is the first ritual that leads to the initiation sacraments, the first set of initiation texts in *The Roman Missal* are the texts for the Rite of Election or Enrollment of Names. The presumption is that if the Rite of Reception into the Order of Catechumens takes place during Mass, the orations from the Mass of the day are used.

The Mass texts for the Election or Enrollment of Names are found under the larger heading: "For the Conferral of the Sacraments of Christian Initiation." Placing the election texts under this heading gives witness to a broader understanding of Christian Initiation that goes beyond the liturgy at which the Sacraments of Initiation are conferred. One learns from these ritual prayers that our initiation into Christ is gradual, marked by stages. In the course of time we pray that the elect may come to the Easter Sacraments "worthily and wisely" (First Scrutiny) and that God "may graciously purify them by the working of this sacrifice" (Prayer over the Offerings, Third Scrutiny).

In the third edition of the Missal we find a rubric that acknowledges that the Rite of Election may take place on another day other than the First Sunday of Lent, in which case these texts for Election or Enrollment of Names may be used. This conforms to the rubric in the *Rite of Christian Initiation of Adults*, which makes provision for celebrating the Rite of Election on a day other than the First Sunday of Lent.[1] What is new is that in addition to these texts we find that the Mass for the Friday of the Fourth Week of Lent may be used as an alternative. A review of these texts reveals their relevance to the initiation process. The Collect for the Mass of Friday in the Fourth Week of Lent says: ". . . grant, we pray, that we may receive / the healing effects with joy . . ." and in the Prayer after Communion we hear: "Grant, we pray, O Lord, / that, as we pass from old to new, / so, with former ways left behind, / we may be renewed in holiness of mind." While these texts are intended for the entire Church, they have a particular meaning for those who are preparing for Christian Initiation. They acknowledge the changes that, with God's grace, we have to make in our lives, if we are to fully embrace the Christian life.

---

1. Cf. RCIA, 128.

The new translation of the Collect for the Rite of Election better captures the need for strength in preparing for Baptism and strength for those who try to live out their Baptism: ". . . look mercifully . . . upon your chosen ones, / that your compassionate and protecting help / may defend both those yet to be born anew / and those already reborn." In the previous translation instead of "strengthen" we find a weaker expression with the words, "continue to bless."

The three orations for the Election and Enrollment of Names will probably not be used frequently, since most dioceses generally celebrate the Rite of Election at the Cathedral Church or at a regional location on a day in Lent that may be other than the First Sunday of Lent and almost always outside of Mass. Nevertheless, the Collect could be used when the Rite of Election is celebrated in the context of a Liturgy of the Word.

There may be pastoral circumstances in some regions where either the Bishop is not able to host a diocesan celebration because of great distances or he may be present in a local parish or principal parish church where he chooses to celebrate the Rite of Election at Mass on the First Sunday of Lent, in which case, these texts are used.

THE CELEBRATION OF THE SCRUTINIES

The presumption is that the Scrutinies are celebrated on the Third, Fourth, and Fifth Sundays of Lent. In addition to the Collect, the Prayer over the Offerings, and the Prayer after Communion, there are special commemorations provided for inclusion in Eucharistic Prayers I, II, and III that are focused on the godparents and the elect. In the 1985 edition of the Missal there was only one commemoration, which was to be inserted into Eucharistic Prayer I. Each commemoration prayer seeks divine assistance for the godparents, who are referred to as servants.

The commemoration for inclusion in Eucharistic Prayer III reads: "Assist your servants with your grace, / O Lord, we pray, / that they may lead these chosen ones by word and example / to a new life in Christ, our Lord." Including the godparents in these ritual prayers at the heart of the Eucharistic Liturgy heightens the role that god-parents play in the formation and initiation of new Christians. In the commemoration for the First Eucharistic Prayer the names of the godparents are read aloud. Eucharistic Prayer I also provides an insert for the *Hanc igitur* ("Therefore, Lord, we pray . . ."):

> graciously accept this oblation
> which we make to you for your servants,
> whom you have been pleased
> to enroll, to choose and call
> for eternal life
> and for the blessed gift of your grace.

While the orations for the Scrutinies were already present in the previous translation of the Missal, they were seldom used because either the Scrutinies were not being celebrated at Sunday Mass or because many priests were unaware that they were in *The Sacramentary* and could be used at the Sunday Masses for the Third, Fourth, and Fifth Sundays of Lent. Unfortunately, the commemoration text to be inserted in the Eucharistic Prayer was printed along with the orations in the Ritual Masses section rather than at the bottom or alongside the Eucharistic Prayer text and so was routinely glossed over. Two of the changes we find in revised Scrutiny Masses is that each Sunday is printed in its entirety and so it more user friendly; and there are now Entrance and Communion Antiphons for each of the three scrutiny Masses when previously there was only one set of antiphons for all three Sundays.

What is characteristic of the revised translation is the stronger language that is used in asking God's favor for the community and the elect.

For example, the Prayer after Communion for the Second Scrutiny in the previous translation reads:

> Lord, be close to your family.
> Rule and guide us on our way to your kingdom
> and bring us to the joy of salvation.

The revised translation reads:

> Sustain your family always in your kindness,
> O Lord, we pray,
> correct them, set them in order,
> graciously protect them under your rule,
> and in your unfailing goodness
> direct them in the way of salvation.

Words and phrases such as "sustain," "correct," "set in order," and "protect" are more reflective of the spirit of the scrutinies and exorcisms found in the RCIA: "The scrutinies are meant to uncover, then heal all that is weak, defective, or sinful in the hearts of the elect; to bring out, then strengthen all that is upright, strong and good."[2]

EASTER VIGIL

Dear brethren (brothers and sisters),
on this most sacred night
in which our Lord Jesus Christ
passed over from death to life,
the Church calls upon her sons and daughters,
scattered throughout the world,
to come together to watch and pray.
If we keep the memorial
of the Lord's paschal solemnity in this way,
listening to his word and celebrating his mysteries,
then we shall have the sure hope
of sharing his triumph over death
and living with him in God.[3]

In this introduction to the Easter Vigil we find the meaning and purpose of the Christian life and the Sacraments of Initiation. We hope to share in Christ's victory over death. We hope to live with Christ in God forever. The baptized and elect who gather in darkness to begin the Easter Vigil have this holy purpose in mind. The baptized will renew their spiritual adoption and the elect will experience for the first time a dying to the old self so as to rise newly born from the waters of life.

The revised translation of the introductory address at the Easter Vigil says "If we keep the memorial of the Lord's paschal solemnity." The previous translation says: "if we honor the memory of his death and resurrection." While this introductory address by the priest can be given "in these or similar words," the revised translation offers a richer understanding of what we are doing at the Easter Vigil when it says "we keep the memorial of the Lord's paschal solemnity."

---

2. RCIA, 141.
3. Introduction to the Easter Vigil.

To "keep the memorial" says more than just to "honor the memory." Keeping the memorial has stronger overtones of the Passover meal (*Pesach*) at which the people of the covenant keep the memorial of the ancient Exodus and Passover. We do more in keeping a memorial than we do in just honoring a memory. Keeping the memorial implies that we are involved in that mystery here and now and that it will have an effect upon us that is just as powerful as the effect it had upon those who first experienced the saving Death and Resurrection of Christ in history.

The full complement of texts for the Paschal Vigil elucidates more fully the mystery of redemption that reaches its climax on this holy night. In the Easter Proclamation (*Exsultet*) the effect of the saving mystery of Christ is boldly sung in the present tense: "The sanctifying power of this night / dispels wickedness, washes faults away, / restores innocence to the fallen, / and joy to mourners." The insertion of the word *sanctifying* before the "power of this night" is noticeable and adds to the divine action underlying what we are experiencing. What is evident in these texts of the Paschal Vigil is that we are being called to holiness by submitting ourselves to the redeeming work of Christ.

The liturgy of the Paschal Vigil is built around the centerpiece of Baptism as the wellspring of our adoption as God's sons and daughters and the promise of eternal life. While the Church confesses her belief in the power of the Cross and the Resurrection of Christ in every act of worship, it is here in the Paschal Vigil that the connection between the Paschal Mystery and the Sacraments of Baptism, Confirmation, and Eucharist are clearly manifested. The saving mystery of Christ is not an abstract theory or theological statement, but the action of God at work to save us. It is through our participation in these sacraments that we are able to appropriate for ourselves the redeeming power of the Passion, Death, and Resurrection of Christ.

The references to Baptism in the Vigil texts are plentiful. These texts come alive when there are candidates for adult Baptism. As the assembly witnesses the Baptism of new members, the mystery of our redemption is manifested before our eyes. The prayer after the seventh reading captures this truth:

> O God of unchanging power and eternal light,
> look with favor on the wondrous mystery of the whole Church

and serenely accomplish the work of human salvation,
which you planned from all eternity;
may the whole world know and see
that what was cast down is raised up,
what has become old is made new,
and all things restored to integrity through Christ,
just as by him they came into being.

The third edition of the Missal appropriately uses the term, "wondrous mystery of the whole Church" by translating the Latin, *ad totius Ecclesiae sacramentum*. The former translation simply read: "look with mercy and favor on your entire Church." The nature of the Church as a sacrament in the world begins here at the Vigil itself as we witness in the baptismal candidates "that what is cast down is raised up." From this starting point the Church must continue to be a witness or sacrament of Christ's redeeming power in the world.

One of the most significant changes in the revised Missal calls for an anointing with the Oil of Catechumens after the renunciation of evil and before the candidates profess their faith. The anointing of the catechumens is done at this point, if it was not already done in the Preparation Rites on Holy Saturday morning. In the United States the anointing with the Oil of Catechumens is anticipated during the Period of the Catechumenate[4] and not employed at the Preparation Rites on Holy Saturday. The anointing may be repeated, however, so it can be used at the Vigil after the renunciation of sin and evil. The insertion of the anointing with the oil of catechumens at this point has its historical roots in the *Apostolic Tradition*. The idea behind the ritual action is that this final renunciation by the elect is sealed tight by the anointing.

A deacon shall bring the oil of exorcism, and shall stand at the presbyter's left hand. . . . Then the presbyter, taking hold of each of those about to be baptized, shall command him to renounce, saying: 'I renounce thee, Satan, and all thy servants and all thy works.' And when he has renounced all these, the presbyter shall anoint him with the oil of exorcism, saying: 'Let all spirits depart far from thee.' Then after these things, let him give him over to the presbyter who baptizes . . . .[5]

---

4. Cf. RCIA, 79, 98–103.

5. *Apostolic Tradition of Hippolytus*, 22, translated by Burton Scott Easton, Archon Books, Cambridge University Press, 1962.

Another significant change in the revised Missal is the
invitation to baptize infants as well as adults at the Easter Vigil. There
is a provision for this in the *Rite of Baptism for Children*, which in fact,
recommends that infant Baptism be celebrated during the Easter
Vigil.[6] As with the adults, the infants would be anointed with the Oil
of Catechumens after the parents have made their renunciation of evil
and their profession of faith. After baptizing the infants the priest
anoints the infants, but not the adults, with sacred chrism. The adults
will be anointed with chrism later in the liturgy when they receive
the Sacrament of Confirmation.

Even when there are no candidates for Baptism, the Vigil
liturgy retains its baptismal focus. In this case the redeeming grace
of Baptism is more directly manifested in the faithful who on this
night solemnly renew their participation in the saving Death and
Resurrection of Christ by renewing their Baptismal vows. The Collect
of the Easter Vigil Mass is inclusive of the already baptized:

> . . . stir up in your Church the spirit of adoption,
> so that, renewed in body and mind,
> we may render you undivided service.

The Collect for the Paschal Vigil is an improvement on
the previous translation, which in part read: "Quicken the spirit
of sonship in your Church." The revised translation, "stir up in your
Church the spirit of adoption," is far more suitable and the use of
inclusive language is welcome.

One could argue that before the Church admits new members
into the Body of Christ through Baptism, it needs first to be renewed
in the same grace. Its first act of "service" will be to pass on the faith
through the Baptism of new members. This is made even more explicit
in the concluding prayer to the Litany of the Saints.

> Almighty ever-living God,
> be present by the mysteries of your great love,
> and send forth the spirit of adoption
> to create the new peoples
> brought to birth for you in the font of Baptism,

---

6. Cf. *Rite of Baptism for Children* (RBC), 9 and 28.

so that what is to be carried out by our humble service
may be brought to fulfillment by your mighty power.

It is interesting to note that in the 1974 edition of the Missal
and in the RCIA there is no concluding prayer to the Litany of Saints.

When there are no candidates for Baptism, the font is not
blessed but a prayer for blessing of water is offered which emphasizes
the renewal of our Baptism.

Therefore, may this water be for us
a memorial of the Baptism we have received,
and grant that we may share
in the gladness of our brothers and sisters
who at Easter have received their Baptism.

The revised translation speaks about the ritual action here as
a "memorial of the Baptism we have received." This is a more thought
provoking image than the previous translation which simply read:
"Let this water remind us of our Baptism." The revised translation
implies a more engaging act of baptismal renewal than simply being
mindful of something that occurred in the past. Notice too that even
though this water blessing is to be used when there are no Baptisms
at the Vigil, there is still a reference to those who are being baptized
in the Church around the world this night. Our celebration of the
Paschal Vigil is intended to keep us united with believers everywhere
who share "in the gladness of our brothers and sisters / who at Easter
have received their Baptism." A final note can be made on the use
of inclusive language in this text. The previous translation read: "let
us share the joys of our brothers / who are baptized this Easter."

BAPTISM

While it remains normative to celebrate adult Baptisms at the Easter
Vigil, the RCIA makes pastoral provision for celebrating adult
Baptism at a time other than the Easter Vigil. There may be pastoral
situations that dictate an exception to the norm. In these cases the
texts for celebrating Baptism at Mass are appropriate. There are two
settings for a ritual Mass for the Conferral of Baptism.

What will be more common than celebrating adult Baptism outside the Easter Vigil will be the celebration of infant Baptism on various Sundays throughout the year. Parishes that choose to celebrate infant Baptism at Sunday Mass will want to consider using these ritual texts. Parishes may not have been aware that these texts were available or that they could be used on many Sundays of the year. It is hoped that once the third edition of the Missal is published these options will be discovered and used when pastorally appropriate. The value in doing so is that the conferral of Baptism at Mass is better integrated into the flow of the entire Mass and provides a succinct theological statement on the sacraments of initiation. The *Rite of Baptism for Children* offers only a brief outline for celebrating the Baptism of infants at Sunday Mass.[7]

Our use of these ritual texts at Sunday Mass is governed by the norms for the Church's calendar. In the 1974 edition of the Missal it states that these texts can be used on any day except the Sundays of Advent, Lent, and Easter, solemnities, Ash Wednesday, and the weekdays of Holy Week. The revised Missal simplifies the rubric by stating that this Mass may be used on days when Ritual Masses are permitted. The rubric adds that when this Ritual Mass is used, the "Penitential Act, the Kyrie, and the Creed are omitted."

Included in the Ritual Mass for the Conferral of Baptism are "commemorations" and "intercessions" for inclusion in Eucharistic Prayers I, II, III, and IV. Eucharistic Prayer I includes a commemoration for the godparents who are to be named in the Eucharistic Prayer. What seems unusual is that while the godparents are remembered by name the neophytes are not named.

During Easter Time, Preface II of Easter may be used and during other liturgical times Preface I for Ordinary Time may be used. The strong baptismal imagery in Preface I of the Sundays in Ordinary Time make this Preface an obvious choice for a ritual Mass of the Conferral of Baptism. Consider the potential for a profound and substantial catechesis based on this Preface text. One can also envision a homily based on this text.

> For through his Paschal Mystery,
> he accomplished the marvelous deed,

---

7. RBC, 29.

by which he has freed us from the yoke of sin and death,
summoning us to the glory of being now called
a chosen race, a royal priesthood,
a holy nation, a people for your own possession,
to proclaim everywhere your mighty works,
for you have called us out of darkness
into your own wonderful light.

What this set of texts suggests is that careful and thoughtful planning ought to be made when celebrating additional rites during Mass. These rites ought not appear as just an appendage that is inserted without a relationship to the rest of the liturgy. What this also suggests is that, in the preparation, attention should be given to the Entrance Antiphon and the Communion Antiphon, which can be sung or music can be selected that reflects the same spirit. For example, the Entrance Antiphon for option B in the texts for the Conferral of Baptism is taken from Titus 3:5–7: "He saved us, not because of deeds done by us in righteousness, but in virtue of his own mercy . . . ." These biblical texts could be used for the homily or a catechesis on the sacrament of Baptism. It is hoped that music composers will look to these Entrance and Communion Antiphons in all the Ritual Masses to create new musical compositions.

Confirmation

When adults or children of catechetical age are baptized they are ordinarily confirmed at the same liturgy. The conferral of Confirmation will most commonly be used when the bishop comes to a parish to celebrate the Sacrament of Confirmation for children or teens who were baptized as infants. Some dioceses also organize special celebrations of Confirmation for adults who for whatever reason missed the being confirmed when they were younger.

There are three settings for Mass texts for the conferral of Confirmation. Option A has two choices for the Collect. While the former translation provided an insert only for Eucharistic Prayer I, the third edition of the Missal provides inserts for Eucharistic Prayers I, II, and III. Preface I or II of the Holy Spirit may be used. The norm for using these texts is the same general rubric that dictates when a Ritual Mass can be celebrated in the course of the liturgical year.

The revised translation has a number of significant changes in the texts, which are theologically and pastorally richer and stronger. For example, in option A, the Prayer over the Gifts in the old translation reads: ". . . send us your Holy Spirit to make us more like Christ in bearing witness to the world." The revised translation for the Prayer over the Offerings reads: ". . . grant that, being conformed more perfectly to your Son, / they may grow steadily in bearing witness to him. . . ." First of all, note that in the previous translation the prayer is made on behalf of all ("send us . . . make us"). In the revised translation the prayer is offered specifically for those who have just been confirmed ("that . . . they may grow"). Secondly, in the 1985 edition of the Missal we pray that we may be "more like Christ," which is more a matter of imitating the example and virtues of Christ. This implies that we imitate Christ in our lives by the help of the Holy Spirit. But the revised translation speaks about the newly confirmed being "conformed more perfectly to your Son." This refers to something that God has done for the candidates in being confirmed. To be "configured to Christ" is a much stronger statement about the effect of the sacrament than the hope that we may be "more like Christ." Our configuration to Christ underscores a permanent change in our lives, traditionally referred to as the "seal" of Confirmation. One can begin to see the potential here for a profound catechesis on the meaning of Confirmation.

EUCHARIST

We know that Eucharist is one of the three Sacraments of Christian Initiation. We recognize most clearly how Eucharist completes our initiation into Christ when, at the Easter Vigil, we witness how the Baptism and Confirmation of the elect culminates at the eucharistic table. When infants are baptized in the Catholic Church in the Latin Rite, however, their Confirmation and reception of the Eucharist is delayed until a later age. This in turn may make the relationship between the Eucharist and the other two Sacraments of Initiation less obvious. Nevertheless, the solemn reception of First Holy Communion does provide the opportunity through catechesis and liturgical celebration to make the intimate link between Baptism, Confirmation, and Eucharist more evident.

Even though the custom of celebrating First Holy Communion is very popular in many countries and celebrated with great solemnity, there is no specific ritual Mass for the reception of First Holy Communion. There are, however, several texts in the Missal that can be used appropriately for this occasion. These texts include a Votive Mass for the Most Holy Eucharist, the Mass texts for the solemnity of the Most Holy Body and Blood of Christ (*Corpus Christi*), the texts from the Evening Mass of the Lord's Supper on Holy Thursday evening, the texts from the Votive Mass of our Lord Jesus Christ, the Eternal High Priest, and two Prefaces of the Most Holy Eucharist. In the older translation the Votive Mass of our Lord Jesus Christ, the Eternal High Priest was published as option B of the Votive Mass of the Holy Eucharist. It now stands as its own Votive Mass.

When would we use these texts in a parish? The most common occasion would be the solemn reception of First Holy Communion for children approaching the Lord's Table for the first time. Whenever Ritual Masses are permitted, these texts can be used as an alternative to the Mass of the day. What is noticeable in all of these texts is a spirituality of the Eucharist that is deeply grounded in the Paschal Mystery (". . . grant that we, who confidently proclaim, under sacramental signs, the Death and Resurrection of Christ"—Collect, Votive Mass of the Most Holy Eucharist) and in the hope of uniting all believers (". . . so that through the Body and Blood of Christ / the whole family of believers may be bound together"—Prayer after Communion, Votive Mass of the Most Holy Eucharist). The references to the Paschal Mystery and to the unity of all believers in the one body of Christ are easily linked to Baptism. While First Communion piety may tend to be very individualistic in tone—"today I receive Jesus in my heart"—the prayer of the Church calls for something far more encompassing. Preface II of the Most Holy Eucharist speaks of our being changed by our reception of the Eucharist: ". . . so that the human race, / bonded by one world, / may be enlightened by one faith / and united by one bond of charity." Preface I of the Most Holy Eucharist says: ". . . as we drink his Blood that was poured out for us, we are washed clean." Granted an eight-year-old child may not be able to adequately grasp the profound mystery of our redemption, but on the other hand, the meaning of the Eucharist as manifested in the prayer of the Church calls for a richer and more comprehensive catechesis than is usually given. Even at eight years old a child can surely understand what it means to live in unity and charity with other Christians. Christ's saving mystery is at work in the celebration of the Eucharist. Children can certainly be taught that Jesus Christ saves us and we do not save ourselves: ". . . for whenever the memorial of this sacrifice is celebrated / the work of our redemption is accomplished" (Prayer over the Offerings, Evening Mass of the Lord's Supper).

In celebrating a First Holy Communion Mass it would be appropriate to include a renewal of Baptismal vows and perhaps a rite of blessing and sprinkling of water. Also, at Communion before the invitation, "Behold, the Lamb of God . . ." the celebrant can offer a special invitation to the communicants highlighting the significance of their First Holy Communion in relationship to the Church and the communicant's desire for God.

Conclusion

The third edition of *The Roman Missal* offers us a rich fare of initiation texts that can inspire catechesis and preaching. Praying these texts over many years will have a profound effect upon our spirituality, provided we have taken the time to ponder their meaning. Pastors and liturgists must work closely together with catechists so that the rites we celebrate will not only become the heartfelt prayer of the Church but its Creed.

The publication of the Missal's new translation and edited texts provides the occasion for parish communities to review the full spectrum of their initiation practice. Although the *Rite of Christian Initiation of Adults* has been promulgated for many years and *The Sacramentary* had already provided complementary texts that reflect the same theological and liturgical vision as found in the RCIA, there are unfortunately some who still regard Christian initiation as an education program culminating in Baptism and Confirmation. One may still hear pastoral ministers referring to the initiation of new Christians as "convert instructions" or "convert classes." This is clearly not what the *Rite of Christian Initiation of Adults* or the texts in *The Roman Missal* envision. One may even find pastors baptizing children of catechetical age or adults with the *Rite of Baptism of Children*. While a thorough catechesis is an essential element in the formation of new Christians, the process of Christian initiation remains a process of conversion and spiritual formation over time within a Christian community and with practical implications for living the Catholic way of life. The publication of the revised initiation texts in *The Roman Missal* is an opportunity to review our pastoral practice to see that we are in fact in sync with the sacramental and pastoral theology embedded in the texts we pray. It is also the occasion to recommit our parish communities to the full implementation of the *Rite of Christian Initiation of Adults* and the celebration of the Sacraments of Initiation as envisioned by the universal Church.

On a practical level, pastors and catechists may have to hone their skills for mystagogical preaching and catechizing. We would do well to review some of the classic examples of mystagogical preaching from the Fathers of the Church, like Saint Cyril of Jerusalem, Saint John Chrysostom, and others, who spoke so eloquently about the divine mysteries.

Making use of all the texts that are available to us undoubtedly requires some time and study in preparation for the liturgy. Priests would be well served by a pastoral staff schooled well enough in the liturgy who can assist them in making appropriate choices from the full deposit of texts found in the Missal and the RCIA.

We can either receive the revised translation of *The Roman Missal* with superficial interest or with an openness to a richer collection of prayers that lend themselves to deeper reflection upon the sacramental mysteries we are privileged to share. Obviously it is the latter that we hope will occur so that the vision of the *Sacrosanctum Concilium* may be realized:

> In the restoration and promotion of the sacred liturgy, this full and active participation by all the people is the aim to be considered before all else; for it is the primary and indispensable source from which the faithful are to derive the true Christian spirit; and therefore pastors of souls must zealously strive to achieve it, by means of the necessary instruction, in all their pastoral work.[8]

---

8. *Sacrosanctum Concilium*, 14.

Chapter 9

The Blessed Virgin Mary in the Third Typical Edition of *The Roman Missal*

Reverend James Presta, STD

Throughout the history of the Church, the Blessed Virgin Mary has occupied a special and unique place in the Church's liturgical and devotional life. What has been woven over the centuries is a beautiful tapestry that links Our Lady with the Paschal Mystery, the Passion, Death, and Resurrection of her divine Son. Mary's presence, in the Sacred Liturgy, weaves together, with golden threads and bright colors, the great tapestry that is salvation history in Jesus Christ.

Mary's role in salvation history is unique. She complements the work of mediation by her Son and she cooperates with the Father's saving plan for all humanity. In Mary, the Church witnesses three mediation events:

> Mary's own cooperation in the redemption of the human race, her distribution of the graces won by the redemption, and her complementary intercession on behalf of the Church.[1]

In this article, I wish to offer a tapestry woven in the liturgical life of the Church in relationship to Mary as it is seen in the Marian Masses of the third typical edition of *The Roman Missal*. The article will review the principal feasts in honor of the Mother of God, as they appear in *The Roman Missal*. I will also explain and examine the new

---

1. Father Neil J. Roy. "Mary and the Liturgical Year." *Mariology: A Guide for Priests, Deacons, Seminarians, and Consecrated Persons.* Mark I. Miravalle, STD (Goleta, California: Queenship Publishing, 2007), page 609.

Votive Masses of the Blessed Mother, on Saturday when no obligatory memorial is assigned to the day. I will also offer a word of explanation on why we devote Saturdays to Our Lady. The article will also offer a general overview of the 46 Masses found in the *Collection of Masses of the Blessed Virgin Mary* that until now, were found in a separate edition of *The Sacramentary*. Some of these Masses have been inserted into the third edition of *The Roman Missal* so that they are more accessible to priests who celebrate and keep sacred the noble tradition of Saturdays in honor of Our Lady.

In beginning this brief introduction of Marian Masses in the third edition of *The Roman Missal,* it must be noted that the Blessed Virgin Mary has long been commemorated in the liturgical life of the Church. It was the documents of Second Vatican Council, particularly chapter 8 of *Lumen Gentium,* and an important reference on the Virgin Mary in *Sacrosanctum Concilium* that sets the tone for Mary's place in the liturgical calendar.

> In celebrating the annual cycle of Christ's mysteries, the Church honors with special love Mary, the Mother of God, who is joined by an inseparable bond to the saving work of her Son.[2]

In an article in Marian Studies, 1989, "The Virgin Mary in the Liturgy: 1963–1988," Father Thomas Thompson, SM, Director of the Marian Library in Dayton, Ohio, highlights the significance of Mary's place in the liturgy since Vatican II. He states that all Marian Feasts, and the Virgin Mary's role in the liturgy "is determined not so much on the number of Marian feasts but on the 'special love' with which the Church honors the Blessed Virgin who is joined by 'an inseparable bond' to the saving work of Christ celebrated and made present in the liturgy." He also stressed the important encyclical of Paul VI, *Marialis Cultus* (1974), which gave rise to Mary's relationship to her Son, Jesus Christ, and to the Church as well as the relation of Marian devotion to liturgy.

The *Collection of Masses of the Blessed Virgin Mary,* published in 1986 by Pope John Paul II, was a completion of the Missal of Paul VI, even though they have been published in two separate volumes: as a *Lectionary for Mass* and a Missal (*The Sacramentary*). The collection was developed as a response to Rectors of Marian Shrines who desired

---

2. *Sacrosanctum Concilium*, 103.

more of a variety in the Marian prayers and Lectionary selections available for special Marian Votive Masses offered for pilgrims who worship at their shrines and places of Marian pilgrimage. Placing Marian liturgy and devotion within the historical dimension of the Second Vatican Council in harmony with the liturgical contributions of both Paul VI and John Paul II is now found in the third typical edition of *The Roman Missal.*[3]

THE PRINCIPAL MARIAN CELEBRATIONS FOUND IN THE ROMAN MISSAL: SOLEMNITIES, FEASTS, OBLIGATORY AND OPTIONAL MEMORIALS

Historically, the weaving of the Marian tapestry in the liturgical life of the Church has its beginnings "after the memorials of the martyrs and the feasts of the apostles."[4] There were no Marian feasts for the first four hundred years. [5] It was the Lord's Day which took precedence in the liturgical life of the early Church. Gradually, with time, however, there developed a rich and deep understanding of Mary's place in "salvation history"[6] and in its liturgical life. In 431 AD, after the Council of Ephesus declared Mary as the "God-bearer," the *Theotokos,* there emerged a sense that Mary should hold a special and venerated place in the Church's liturgical and devotional life. Thus, Marian feasts were established, especially in the "Holy Land, where memories of Mary still remained."[7]

After the Council of Ephesus in 431 AD Pope Sixtus III (432–40) built a basilica in Mary's honor, which subsequently was called Saint Mary Major.[8] Like Churches in the East, the West

3. Thomas A. Thompson, sm. "The Virgin Mary in the Liturgy; 1963–1988." *Marian Studies,* proceedings of the Fortieth National Convention of the Mariology Society of America held in Burlingame, CA, May 31 and June 1, 1989. Ed. T. A. Koehler. Vol. XL (Dayton, Ohio: Mariological Society of America, 1989), page 98.

4. Verlag Herder. *Das Kirchenjahr mitfeiern: Seine Geschichte und seine Bedeutung nach der Liturgieereuerung.* Trans. by Adolf Adam (New York, NY: Pueblo Publishing Co., Inc., 1981), page 212.

5. J. D. Crichton. *Our Lady in the Liturgy* (Collegeville, Minnesota: Liturgical Press, 1997), page 23.

6. Ibid.

7. Ibid.

8. Kilian McDonnell, osb. "The Marian Liturgical Tradition." Ed. H. George Anderson, J. Francis Stafford, and Joseph A. Burges. *The One Mediator, the Saints, and Mary: Lutherans and Catholics in Dialogue VIII* (Minneapolis, Minnesota: Augsburg Fortress, 1992), pages 177–191.

wanted to relate the Marian cult to Christmas Time. The Church found a liturgical link with the Blessed Virgin Mary by using certain aspects of the liturgy of virgins for the newly developed cult of Mary. The liturgy of virgins became an essential ingredient for the development of texts for Marian liturgical celebration. "The introduction of new feast from the East eventually made the generic feasts of Mary (January 1) disappear from the calendar."[9]

The Marian liturgies in the early "Church drew heavily on the liturgy of virgins."[10] This means that the doctrinal emphasis in the Marian liturgies would be on the virginity of Mary. This explains why the Church often uses the bridal imagery for its Marian feasts. This particular image of Mary is also an image used in reference to the Church as the Bride of Christ. Therefore, the bridal themes are used in Marian liturgies as well as incarnational texts which are reflective of the Advent and Christmas Time

It appears that the first feast of Mary was the Assumption, or the Dormition of Our Lady, around 450 AD. This feast occupied a special place in the East and eventually, by the sixth century, "Emperor Justinian ordered the celebration of the feast throughout the empire."[11]

By the seventh century, the Church of Rome would incorporate the East's tradition of celebrating Mary's Dormition, recording it in the *Liber Pontificalis*. Pope Hadrian, a century later, would insert in his Sacramentary, the Assumption of Our Lady.[12] It should also be noted that the *Leonine Sacramentary* of the seventh century and the *Gelasian* of the eighth century mention Mary with some frequency.[13]

My purpose here is not to give a history of Mary's liturgical feasts throughout the centuries, but to offer one of the original golden threads in this Marian tapestry that the Church has so exquisitely woven into its liturgical books. Namely, this first feast of Mary in the East and the West, the Dormition (the Assumption), will usher in a plethora of Marian feasts that will enrich the liturgical life of the Church throughout the centuries.

9. Ibid., page 180.
10. Ibid., page 187.
11. Chrichton, page 24.
12. Ibid., page 24.
13. McDonnell, page 180.

In fact, fast forwarding the liturgical "clock" some 1,600 years later, here listed are the solemnities, feasts and memorials incorporated into the third typical edition of *The Roman Missal*:

- January 1: Solemnity of Mary, the Holy Mother of God
- February 2: Feast of the Presentation of the Lord
- February 11: Optional Memorial of Our Lady of Lourdes
- March 25: Solemnity of the Annunciation of the Lord
- May 13: Our Lady of Fatima
- May 31: Feast of the Visitation of the Blessed Virgin Mary
- Immaculate Heart of Mary: Saturday following the Second Sunday after Pentecost
- July 16: Optional Memorial of Our Lady of Mount Carmel
- August 5: Optional Memorial of the Dedication of the Basilica of St. Mary Major
- August 15: Solemnity of the Assumption of the Blessed Virgin Mary
- August 22: Memorial of the Queenship of the Blessed Virgin Mary
- September 8: Feast of the Nativity of the Blessed Virgin Mary
- September 12: Memorial of the Most Holy Name of Mary
- September 15: Memorial of Our Lady of Sorrows
- October 7: Memorial of Our Lady of the Rosary
- November 21: Memorial of the Presentation of the Blessed Virgin Mary
- December 8: Solemnity of the Immaculate Conception of the Blessed Virgin Mary
- December 12: Our Lady of Guadalupe

Before the Second Vatican Council, the Popes of the twentieth century sought to make Christ the center and focus of the Church's liturgical calendar, especially the precedence of Sunday as the Lord's Day. For example, in 1913, "Pius X began to displace Marian observances that occurred on Sundays."[14] Even Pius XII and John XXIII sought to make Marian feasts optional. These Marian feasts were relegated to local calendars for their celebration, since they were moveable feasts.

The Roman Missal of Pope John XXIII in 1962 would allow "sixteen proper formularies" for the feasts of Mary that would be celebrated locally by religious orders and societies.

---

14. Roy, STD, page 651.

By 1969, the Missal of Paul VI reduced the Marian feasts on the liturgical calendar to thirteen. They break down by liturgical ranking as follows.

Three Solemnities

- January 1: Mary, Holy Mother of God
- August 15: Assumption
- December 8: Immaculate Conception

Two Feasts

- May 31: Visitation
- September 8: Nativity of the Blessed Virgin Mary

Four Obligatory Memorials:

- August 22: Queenship of Mary
- September 15: Our Lady of Sorrows
- October 7: Our Lady of the Rosary
- November 2: Presentation of Mary

Optional Memorials:

- February 11: Our Lady of Lourdes
- Immaculate Heart of Mary (Saturday after solemnity of the Most Sacred Heart)
- July 16: Our Lady of Mount Carmel
- August 5: Dedication of Saint Mary Major

Two optional memorials were added to the third typical edition of *The Roman Missal*:

- May 13: Our Lady of Fatima
- September 12: Most Holy Name of Mary

Also the Immaculate Heart of Mary has been raised to the rank of an obligatory memorial. Pope John Paul II had a great devotion to Our Lady of Fatima since it was on her feast that he was spared death after an assassination attempt was made on his life on May 13, 1981.

Pope John Paul II also added Our Lady of Guadalupe to the general Roman calender, raising its rank to optional memorial. In the Church of the Americas, however, this Marian feast has been raised to the rank of feast, *Nuestra Señora de Guadalupe*.

COMMON OF THE BLESSED VIRGIN MARY

The number of votive Masses in honor of the Blessed Virgin Mary has been expanded from five in the 1969 Missal to eight, in the third edition of *The Roman Missal* which also includes Masses for Advent, Christmas Time, Lent, and Easter Time in memory of the Mother of the Lord.

There are the beautiful golden strands added to the Marian tapestry of the Church's liturgical life in the third edition of *The Roman Missal*. They are Votive Masses of the Blessed Virgin Mary inspired by Pope Paul VI and his 1974 Apostolic Exhortation *Marialis Cultus*. These golden liturgical threads are the same as those found in the *Collection of Masses of the Blessed Virgin Mary*.

The Common of the Blessed Virgin Mary in the third edition of *The Roman Missal* have been enriched by the following Marian themes found in the Masses:
- Mary, Mother of the Church
- Holy Name of Mary
- Mary, Queen of the Apostles

COLLECTION OF THE MASSES OF THE BLESSED VIRGIN MARY

It is not possible to extol enough the riches and beauty that these 46 Masses offer the Church in its liturgical commemoration of the Mother of God.

Here listed are the 46 Masses found in the Collection. In the footnotes, I have provided a quote from the particular Mass to show the richness of these Masses.

Advent[15]

1. The Blessed Virgin Mary, Chosen Daughter of Israel
2. The Blessed Virgin Mary and the Annunciation of the Lord
3. The Visitation of the Blessed Virgin Mary

---

15. Thompson, page 98.

Christmas Time

4. Mary, Holy Mother of God
5. The Blessed Virgin Mary, Mother of the Savior
6. The Blessed Virgin Mary and the Epiphany of the Lord
7. The Blessed Virgin Mary and the Presentation of the Lord
8. Our Lady of Nazareth
9. Our Lady of Cana

Lent

10. Holy Mary, Disciple of the Lord
11. The Blessed Virgin Mary at the Foot of the Cross, I
12. The Blessed Virgin Mary at the Foot of the Cross, II
13. The Commending of the Blessed Virgin Mary
14. The Blessed Virgin Mary, Mother of the Reconciliation

Easter Time

15. The Blessed Virgin Mary and the Resurrection of the Lord
16. Holy Mary, Fountain of Light and Life
17. Our Lady of the Cenacle
18. The Blessed Virgin Mary, Queen of the Apostles

Ordinary Time

Section 1. Celebration of the Mother of God under titles chiefly from Scripture or that express Mary's bond with the Church.

19. Holy Mary, Mother of the Lord
20. Holy Mary, the New Eve
21. The Holy Name of the Blessed Virgin Mary
22. Holy Mary, Handmaid of the Lord[16]
23. The Blessed Virgin Mary, Temple of the Lord
24. The Blessed Virgin Mary, Seat of Wisdom
25. The Blessed Virgin Mary, Image and Mother of the Church, I
26. The Blessed Virgin Mary, Image and Mother of the Church, II
27. The Blessed Virgin Mary, Image and Mother of the Church, III

---

16. Ibid., page 98.

28. The Immaculate Heart of the Blessed Virgin Mary
29. The Blessed Virgin Mary, Queen of All Creation

Section 2. Memorials of the Blessed Virgin Mary under the titles that refer to her cooperation in fostering the spiritual life of the faithful.

30. The Blessed Virgin Mary, Mother and Mediatrix of Grace
31. The Blessed Virgin Mary, Fountain of Salvation
32. The Blessed Virgin Mary, Mother and Teacher in the Spirit
33. The Blessed Virgin Mary, Mother of Good Counsel
34. The Blessed Virgin Mary, Cause of Our Joy
35. The Blessed Virgin Mary, Pillar of Faith
36. The Blessed Virgin Mary, Mother of Fairest Love
37. The Blessed Virgin Mary, Mother of Divine Hope
38. Holy Mary, Mother of Unity

Section 3. Memorials of the Blessed Virgin under titles that suggest her compassionate intercession on behalf of the faithful.

39. Holy Mary, Queen and Mother of Mercy
40. The Blessed Virgin Mary, Mother of Divine Providence
41. The Blessed Virgin Mary, Mother of Consolation
42. The Blessed Virgin Mary, Help of Christians
43. Our Lady of Ransom
44. The Blessed Virgin Mary, Health of the Sick
45. The Blessed Virgin Mary, Queen of Peace
46. The Blessed Virgin Mary, Gate of Heaven

Advent

• The Visitation of the Blessed Virgin Mary[17]

---

17. *Collection of Masses of the Blessed Virgin Mary*, Volume I. Sacramentary (New York, New York: Catholic Book Publishing Company, 1992), page 36. "On more than one occasion the Roman liturgy celebrates the grace-filled mystery in the unfolding of salvation when the Virgin Mary, overshadowed by the Holy Spirit and bearing the Word of God, visits Elizabeth: on the feast itself (31 May) before the solemnity of the Birth of John the Baptist (24 June); during Advent, because of its close connection with the solemnity of Christmas, and in particular on the Fourth Sunday of Advent of Year C.

Christmas Time

- Holy Mary, Mother of God[18]

Lent

- The Blessed Virgin Mary at the Foot of the Cross[19]

Easter Time

- The Blessed Virgin Mary, Queen of Apostles[20]

Ordinary Time: Section I

- The Blessed Virgin Mary, Seat of Wisdom[21]
- The Blessed Virgin Mary, Image and Mother of the Church[22]
- The Blessed Virgin Mary, Queen of all Creation[23]

---

18. Ibid., page 43. "The texts of this Mass echo the writings of the Fathers of the Church and ancient liturgical prayers, and in particular: the thought of Saint Augustine . . . the sayings of St. Bernard."

19. Ibid., page 65. "the prayers of the Mass recall the plan of salvation, by which God joined the suffering of the mother with the suffering of her Son" (Opening Prayer).

20. Ibid., page 84. "This Mass, apart from the preface, is taken from the [Proper of Masses of the Society of the Catholic Apostolate . . .]. This formulary has great missionary value. The assembly of the faithful prays that the Church may spread 'the glory of [God's] name in our words and actions' [Opening Prayer], may 'spread throughout the world' [Prayer over the Gifts], and 'may always advance in the way of salvation' [Prayer after Communion]."

21. Ibid., page 204. "The title 'seat of Wisdom' celebrates the maternal role of our Lady, her royal dignity, an her incomparable wisdom and prudence in the things of God . . . ."

22. Page 14, article 6: "Masses of the Blessed Virgin Mary have their meaning and purpose from her close participation in the history of salvation. Therefore, when the Church commemorates the role of the Mother of the Lord, in the work of redemption or honors her privileges, it is above all celebrating the events of salvation in which, by God's salvific plan, the Blessed Virgin was involved in view of the mystery of Christ." Page 19, article 20: "The *Collection of Masses of the Blessed Virgin Mary* is made up of principally of the texts for Marian Masses that are found in the propers of the particular churches or of religious institutes or in *The Roman Missal (Sacramentary)*." Page 18, article 21: "The *Collection of Masses* is intended for: Marian shrines where Masses of the Blessed Virgin Mary are celebrated frequently, in accord with the provisions to be indicated in nos. 29–33; ecclesial communities that on the Saturdays in Ordinary Time desire to celebrate a Mass of the Blessed Virgin, in accord with the provision to be indicated in no. 34."

23. Ibid., page 218. "Our Lady is *the queen gloriously reigning in heaven*, because she was on earth the lowly handmaid . . . . She is *queen and mother*, because she became the mother of the messianic King, who sits 'on the throne of David and rules over his kingdom . . . ' She is *the queen who intercedes*, exalted 'above all the choirs of angels,' reigning in glory with her Son, interceding for all God's children our advocate of grace, and the queen of all creation. . . . She is *the queen who is the sign of the Church in its future glory*, because what has been

Ordinary Time: Section II

- The Blessed Virgin Mary, Mother of Good Counsel[24]
- The Blessed Virgin Mary, Cause of Our Joy[25]

MASSES OF THE BLESSED VIRGIN MARY IN THE THIRD EDITION OF *THE ROMAN MISSAL:* A COMMENTARY ON THE NEW MARIAN ORATIONS

To offer a sampling, or another rich and colorful strand of thread to this tapestry of Our Lady in the liturgy, here is a short commentary on the richness of the Marian texts in the third edition of *The Roman Missal*.

January 1: The Solemnity of Mary, Holy Mother of God

Before 1969, on January 1, we celebrated the feast of the Circumcision of Jesus. In the Missal of Pope Paul VI, the ancient solemnity of Mary, the Holy Mother of God was reinstated.

In the 1969 Missal, the opening Collect states, "God our Father, may we always profit by the prayers of the Virgin Mary, for you bring us life and salvation through Jesus Christ her Son."

The third edition of *The Roman Missal* emphasizes Mary's "fruitful virginity" and recognizes Mary's intercessory role, for she is the woman "through whom we were found worthy / to receive the author of life, / our Lord Jesus Christ, your Son."

In the Collect, the new Missal offers a more explicit reason for our worship on this solemnity of Mary, the Holy Mother of God, as the Church concludes the Octave of Christmas.

---

accomplished in her as a member surpassing all others will be accomplished in all the members of Christ's Mystical Body."

24. Ibid., page 47. "In the Mass text our Lady, enlightened by the gift of counsel, is honored as mother and teacher as she cries out in gratitude in the words of Wisdom itself . . . . In celebrating this Mass we earnestly ask God for the gift of counsel, to teach us how to know his will and to guide us in all we do."

25. Ibid., page 51. "The texts of this Mass recall the saving actions of God through Christ in the Holy Spirit that have brought joy to the Blessed Virgin or to the Church or to humanity."

February 2: The Feast of the Presentation of the Lord

Joseph and Mary take Jesus to the Temple and Simeon and the prophetess Anna speak of the role this child would play in the future of his People. While not a Marian feast, Mary does figure prominently in this text.

Rightfully so, the Prefaces of both the 1969 and 2001 Missals place the focus on Jesus, "the glory of Israel and Light of the nations."

March 25: The Solemnity of the Annunciation of the Lord

The Annunciation is closely tied to the celebration of the Nativity of the Lord on December 25. The solemnity is really a Christological more than a Marian feast in nature.

In the third edition of the Missal, the Preface for the Annunciation, which focuses on the Virgin Mary conceiving Jesus by the power of the Holy Spirit, also emphasizes Mary whose immaculate womb has been preserved for the Savior of the world and who will "lovingly" bear him so that, "the promises to the children of Israel might come about / and the hope of nations be accomplished beyond all telling."

July 16: Optional Memorial of Our Lady of Mount Carmel

In the Collect for this Carmelite observance of Mary, the third edition of *The Roman Missal* improves the wording of the 1969 Missal which asks that the "prayer of the Virgin Mary protect us."

The revised text offers a more appropriate and exact visual for this observance of Mary on "Mount" Carmel:

> May the venerable intercession of the glorious Virgin Mary come to our aid, we pray, O Lord, so that, fortified by her protection, we may reach the mountain which is Christ.

August 5: Optional Memorial of the Dedication of the Basilica of St. Mary Major

A change in emphasis is offered in the third edition of the Missal for this optional memorial of Our Lady of the Snow which states that "we cannot please you by our own deeds, / may be saved through the intercession of the Mother of your Son and Lord." The 1969 Missal does not use the word "intercession" in its opening prayer as does the new translation in the third edition of the Missal. Therefore, the new Missal accentuates our belief that Mary's powerful intercessory prayers on behalf of her children can aid us on the road to eternal salvation.

August 15: Solemnity of the Assumption of the Blessed Virgin Mary

In the third edition of the Missal, the opening Collect for the Vigil Mass of the Assumption reminds the faithful that Mary was crowned "with surpassing glory," and with the prayers of Glorious Virgin Mary assumed into the Heaven, that "saved by the mystery of your redemption, / we may merit to be exalted by you on high."

The link between the saving power of Christ's Resurrection and Mary's Assumption is given a voice in today's liturgy, reminding us that Mary's Assumption is among the first fruits of the Resurrection. Again, there is a clearer articulation of what we believe about Mary's Assumption in the new Missal compared with the 1969 edition:

> rightly you would not allow her
> to see the corruption of the tomb
> since from her own body she marvelously brought forth
> your incarnate Son, the Author of all life.

The 1969 Missal states "you would not allow **decay** to touch her body" (emphasis added). This new emphasis that she does not "corrupt the tomb" versus no "decay to touch her body" reminds us that, "whether Mary died or not, she was not subject to the law of death, which is the corruption of the body in the grave . . . . A concrete indication of belief in the Assumption of Mary, is found in the fact that the Church has never looked for the bodily relics of the Blessed Virgin nor proposed them for veneration."[26]

September 8: Feast of the Nativity of the Blessed Virgin Mary

Rather than use the word "birth," the Collect in the third edition of the Missal uses the precise word "Nativity" for the feast of Mary's

---

26. Paul Haffner. *The Mystery of Mary* (Chicago, Illinois: Liturgy Training Publications, 2004), page 218.

birth. Again, the emphasis of the third edition of the Missal warrants the exact name of the prayer to be used in the Collect of this feast. It reminds the faithful why we have gathered to offer praise and thanks to God the Father for the Nativity of Our Lady.

September 12: Memorial of the Most Holy Name of Mary

This Marian observance was added to the third edition of the Missal to remind the faithful that as we venerate the holy name of Mary, the Mother of God, we give glory and honor to the Father for the name of his only-begotten Son, Jesus, whose optional memorial (the Holy Name of Jesus) is now celebrated in the third edition of the Missal on January 3. There is a great link between the names of Jesus and Mary and now the Church commemorates the greatness of their holy names within the liturgical calendar.

September 15: Memorial of Our Lady of Sorrows

As the third Marian observance within this Octave of Marian feasts (September 8, Nativity of the Blessed Virgin Mary and September 12, the Most Holy Name of Mary), there is an emphasis to state the name of the feast in the prayers of the Mass. In this case, the Prayer after Communion states that the faithful recall "how the Blessed Virgin Mary suffered with her Son" on this day.

October 7: Memorial of Our Lady of the Rosary

For the memorial of Mary's Rosary, the Collect of the third edition of the Missal shifts from the wording of the 1969 Missal which emphasizes the revelation by an angel of Christ's coming as man to a prayer quite familiar to those who frequently pray the Rosary. The Collect now used in the Missal is adopted from the concluding prayer used in the recitation of the Rosary by the faithful.

> Pour forth, we beseech you, O Lord,
> your grace into our hearts,
> that we, to whom the Incarnation of Christ your Son
> was made known by the message of an Angel,
> may, through the intercession of the Blessed Virgin Mary,

by his Passion and Cross
be brought to the glory of his Resurrection.
Through . . . .

December 8: Solemnity of the Immaculate Conception of the Blessed Virgin Mary

In the Collect of today's solemnity the name of this observance is stated as "Immaculate Conception of the Blessed Virgin." So too, in the Prayer over the Gifts, "we offer you, O Lord, / on the Solemnity of the Immaculate Conception / of the Blessed Virgin Mary."

The 1969 Missal refers to her as the "sinless" Virgin Mary in both the collect and the Prayer over the Gifts.

WHY SATURDAYS IN HONOR OF OUR LADY?

The answer to this question lies in the tradition of the Church. Legend tells us that Jesus appeared to Mary on the Saturday after his death. Another custom comes from the Church of Rome. Jean Frisk offers these reflections from the Mary Page Web site, that, on the Saturday before White Sunday, "the newly baptized members of the Church were led from Saint John's baptistry of the Lateran to Mary's great shrine on the Esquilin, St. Mary Major."[27]

By the eighth century, the great Marian Church of the East celebrated Our Lady on Saturday. The liturgical books of the ninth and tenth centuries contain Masses in honor of the Blessed Virgin Mary.

Another hint in tradition which helps our understanding of the liturgical relationship between Our Lady and Saturday lies in the great Benedictine monk Alcuin (735–804) who composed votive Masses for each day of the week, including two Masses to Our Lady on Saturday.

Various religious orders also fostered the link between Mary and Saturdays by celebrating special Masses in her honor. For example, the Dominicans in the fifteenth century encouraged devotion to Our Lady with a hymn which sung that, when creation was completed on Saturday, this gave reason to celebrate the fulfillment of God's plan of

27. Jean Frisk, "Mary Page," available from http://campus.udayton.edu/mary/; Accessed February 11, 2010.

Salvation, realized through Mary and ultimately, her only Son, Jesus. Ultimately, "the Church encourages the venerable tradition of observing Our Lady's Saturday as a bridge from the week to the Lord's day."[28]

Mary leads us to her Son in salvation history. So too, on Saturdays, in the liturgical life of the Church, Mary prepares us for the unfolding of the Paschal Mystery each and every Sunday in the Church's Liturgy.

CONCLUSION

In this article, an attempt was made to analyze and explain the new Votive Masses of 2002. The argument can certainly be made that the increased number of Marian texts available in the third typical edition of *The Roman Missal* is a mirror and a reflection of the great Marian devotion and spirituality of our late Pontiff, Pope John Paul II. His insertion of the optional memorial of Our Lady of Fatima (May 13) on the Roman calendar as well as the fact that he raised the rank for the Immaculate Heart of Mary from optional to obligatory memorial demonstrates the late Pontiff's filial gratitude and deep appreciation to the Virgin of Fatima for saving his life in the assassination attempt in St. Peter's Square on May 13, 1981.

Pope John Paul the Great has left his *Totus Tuus* mark on the third typical edition of *The Roman Missal*. The Church will greatly benefit in the future from these beautiful Marian texts that will enhance and promote the Marian devotional and liturgical life of the Church and its relationship with Jesus Christ, the center of our worship.

This article also offered some rationale for the Church's tradition in honoring Mary on Saturdays. The Saturdays of Our Lady prepare us for the great Sunday celebration of the Lord's Resurrection. Mary always leads us to Christ and this is most evident in the Church's liturgical calendar.

The new and improved wording of the texts found in the third typical edition of *The Roman Missal* will provide a more exact and articulate understanding of the Blessed Mother's role in the Church today. The Church looks to Mary for her maternal intercession and she is "ever present as the mother of the Church and its

28. Roy, page 664.

advocate."[29] The Church identifies itself with Mary, as it celebrates liturgy in union with and in imitation of her. If we imitate Mary, we become more fully conformed to Jesus. "Participation in liturgy with and like Mary can be 'the most excellent homage of devotion' offered to her."[30]

> Mary always leads the faithful to a greater knowledge and deeper appreciation of her Son. Of Mary there can never be enough, since she brings us to ever deeper levels of Christ.[31]

Mary is the type of the Church . . . exemplar of both virgin and mother. She is the model for the Church living out the Paschal Mystery. She is the "*Virgo audiens . . . orans . . . pariens . . . offerens vigilans* . . . . She listens and keeps the word . . . praises and thanks God . . . manifests Christ . . . prays and intercedes for all . . . generates and nourishes the life of grace . . . offers Christ to the Father and offers himself . . . waits and watches for the coming of the Lord."[32]

Over the centuries, there are many golden threads sewn into the tapestry of the Church's liturgical life regarding the Blessed Virgin Mary and her relation to her divine Son, Jesus Christ and his holy bride, the Church. The third typical edition of *The Roman Missal* highlights the following Marian themes throughout the year:

- Mary's revelation to the Holy Spirit, the Church and humanity;
- Mary as Premier disciple;
- Mary as Exemplar of the Church at worship;
- Mary as Model of faith;
- Mary as the New Woman.

In conclusion, I offer these thoughts which are taken from the epilogue of Christopher O'Donnell, OCARM, *At Worship with Mary: A Pastoral and Theological Study.*

> As we celebrate the festivals of Mary, we constantly hear her words. 'The almighty has done great things for me, holy is his name.' Our liturgical celebrations, and our theological and prayerful reflections, allow us to join in Mary's praise of God's goodness to her, and through her also to us.

---

29. *Collection of Masses for the Blessed Virgin Mary*, 12.
30. Thompson, page 103.
31. Roy, page 665.
32. Thompson, page 91.

But the liturgical observances of Mary have perhaps another role also. As we struggle forward on our pilgrim way, we cannot but be conscious of the cross, of the weight of sin, of difficulties in discipleship. The figure of Mary is a vision of beauty; it does not threaten; it only draws us on. Her liturgical observances are moments of repose and refreshment on our journey. Beauty cannot be possessed; it can only be enjoyed. In a frenetic world, we need moments of tranquility. In times of stress and anxiety, we need to raise our eyes aloft. The way of beauty is an authentic approach to Mary, as Pope Paul VI told the Seventh Mariological and Fourteenth Marian Congresses. It is also a way for all theology and for all spirituality.

Celebration of Mary can encourage us to move from admiration of her beauty to marvel also at our own. God's faithful love has enriched us also. In a lower key Mary's song of praise is the Church's as well: 'The Almighty has done great things for me, holy is his name.'[33]

---

33. Luke 1:49.

Chapter 10

The Gift of Song: Music and the New English Translation of the Third Typical Edition of *The Roman Missal*

Jerry Galipeau, DMIN

> God has bestowed upon his people the gift of song. God dwells within each human person, in the place where music takes its source. Indeed, God, the giver of song, is present whenever his people sing his praises.[1]

This is the very first line of *Sing to the Lord: Music in Divine Worship*. This document, which guides the pastoral music ministry for the Church in the United States, begins by naming God as the "giver of song."[2] When God's people gather to offer praise and thanks at the celebration of Mass—when we lift up our voices in song—there is most definitely a holy exchange of gifts. We use the gift of song to praise, thank, and give glory to the very giver of that gift.

This essay has been written from my own perspective as a Catholic music publisher, a pastoral musician, and a practicing "pew Catholic."

THE INFLUENCE OF *SING TO THE LORD: MUSIC IN DIVINE WORSHIP*

Sing to the Lord: Music in Divine Worship, a revision of *Music in Catholic Worship*, was developed by the Committee on Divine Worship of the

---

1. *Sing to the Lord: Music in Divine Worship* (STL), 1.
2. Ibid.

United States Conference of Catholic Bishops (USCCB). On November 14, 2007, the Latin Church members of the USCCB approved these guidelines. These guidelines are designed to provide direction to those preparing for the celebration of the Sacred Liturgy according to the current liturgical books (in the ordinary form of celebration). [3]

So begins the introduction to this fairly new document, meant to guide the ministry of liturgical music in the United States. While this chapter cannot do justice to the entire breadth of this document, some sections are critical as the Church begins the implementation of the new English translation of the *Missale Romanum.*

The Second Vatican Council's call for full, conscious, and active participation in the liturgy is echoed in *Sing to the Lord.* "Singing is one of the primary ways that the assembly of the faithful participates actively in the Liturgy . . . The musical formation of the assembly must be a continuing concern in order to foster full, conscious, and active participation." [4] One of the challenges to be faced as the new translation is implemented is this "musical formation of the assembly." Too many, I believe, think of music as an "add-on" to the Mass. A real challenge as we teach new and revised musical settings of the Mass is to teach people that the Mass itself is musical by its very nature. One of the ways this can be achieved is to reinforce or begin to pay attention to some of the principles outlined in *Sing to the Lord.*

Sing to the Lord focuses on an important principle also named in the *General Instruction of the Roman Missal* (GIRM): the dialogues and the acclamations are the most important elements to be sung at the Church's liturgy. "Since the celebration of Mass by its nature has a 'communitarian' character, both the dialogues between the Priest and the assembled faithful, and the acclamations are of great significance; for they are not simply outward signs of communal celebration but foster and bring about communion between Priest and people." [5] By their nature, they are short and uncomplicated and easily invite active participation by the entire assembly. Every effort should therefore be made to introduce or strengthen as a normative practice the singing of the dialogues between the priest, deacon, lector, or reader, and the people. Even a priest with very limited singing ability is capable of

3. See STL, 1.
4. Ibid., 26.
5. *General Instruction of the Roman Missal* (GIRM), 34.

chanting "The Lord be with you" on a single pitch.[6] The singing of
the dialogues has not been a part of the liturgical experience of most
Roman Catholics. In my own parish, at the beginning of Advent of
2009, the parish liturgy committee urged our pastor to begin chanting
the Sign of the Cross and the greeting at the Introductory Rites of
the Mass. He already regularly chants the Preface Dialogue and the
Preface. We had spent time studying the *General Instruction of the
Roman Missal*, sharing the rich theology posited there with regard to
the greeting at the beginning of Mass. "When the Entrance Chant is
concluded, the Priest stands at the chair and, together with the whole
gathering, signs himself with the Sign of the Cross. Then by means
of the Greeting he signifies the presence of the Lord to the assembled
community. By this greeting and the people's response, the mystery of
the Church gathered together is made manifest."[7] When we shared this
at our liturgy committee meetings, many expressed surprise that the
greeting held so much importance; so much theological weight. This
might be due to the fact that in too many parishes, it is substituted or
augmented by a hearty "Good morning, everybody." This kind of
familiar greeting, in my opinion, waters down the richness of what is
being expressed here: the signification of the "presence of the Lord" and
the manifestation of "the mystery of the Church gathered together."[8]

When we implemented this change in the parish, the music
director rehearsed it with the people before Mass, sharing the reasons
why we made the decision to move in this direction. He helped all
of those gathered to understand that this moment is not a "Hi, how
are you?" "Fine, and you?" moment. He told us that it is a profound
announcement that what we are doing is all about naming Christ as
our Lord and announcing his presence right at the beginning of Mass.
When the pastor first began chanting these elements, it was awkward
and people were hesitant. But it did not take long for us to make this
part of our regular practice. That practice has now been occurring for
nearly a year. Frankly, I can't imagine our pastor and our community
not singing this now. It has simply become a part of the fabric of our
prayer. There is an important lesson to be learned as we begin the
implementation of the new translation. Members of the assembly will

6. STL, 115a.
7. GIRM, 50.
8. Ibid.

need leaders who will explain the significance of new words. Liturgical and musical leaders will need to take time to explain and rehearse new musical settings of new words.

In the new English translation of the *Missale Romanum*, the newly translated words "And with your spirit" will cause some difficulty on the part of the members of the assembly. Following years of the lived experience of the liturgy, Catholics just naturally respond "And also with you" when greeted with "The Lord be with you." Following *Sing to the Lord*'s recommendation that the dialogues be sung may be a way to make the change much less jarring for people. I would contend that if parishes begin singing these dialogues beginning the very first Sunday that the new translation is prayed, the transition will be much smoother than if they were to be recited.

I anticipate that approximately sixty revised and new musical settings will have "hit the holy streets" when music publishers are given the go-ahead to publish these new and revised settings. *Sing to the Lord* addresses the issue of the capabilities of learning music by congregations.

> So that the holy people may sing with one voice, the music must be within its members' capability. Some congregations are able to learn more quickly and will desire more variety. Others will be more comfortable with a stable number of songs so that they can be at ease when they sing. Familiarity with a stable repertoire of liturgical songs rich in theological content can deepen the faith of the community through repetition and memorization. A pastoral judgment must be made in all cases.[9]

Parish musicians would be wise to create long-range preparations to implement new musical settings in the parish. Perhaps two or three musical settings of the dialogues and acclamations are enough for the first several years of the celebration of the Mass with the revised translations. Many music directors currently choose a musical setting of the eucharistic acclamations (Preface Dialogue, Sanctus, Memorial Acclamation, great Amen) for consistent use throughout a particular liturgical time. This helps the assembly experience the integrity of the liturgical time. Music directors and those who prepare the liturgy might take the long view, choosing the musical settings they plan to implement over a period of several years. The wisdom from

---

9. STL, 27.

Sing to the Lord is helpful here. Many parishioners will be jarred by the revised translation. Overwhelming them with many new or revised musical settings won't be particularly helpful.

Preparation of a Music Publisher

As the associate publisher at World Library Publications (WLP), the music and liturgy division of the J. S. Paluch Company, it is my responsibility to ensure that we are serving the needs of the singing and praying Church. The introduction of the revised English translation of the *Missale Romanum* is the greatest single event to affect the work of this publishing house since the years following the Second Vatican Council. It was largely the work of the J. S. Paluch Company during the years following the Council that helped people pray the Mass in English. Through its many publications, the company assisted the Church in that time of great transition. It is once again our responsibility to assist the Church in this next moment of transition.

I have decided to present this section of the chapter in narrative form, telling the story of one music publisher as we have addressed the issues of the new translation over the past several years. When I began my own work at WLP eleven years ago, I was responsible for editing the various English-language worship resources. Within the first few years, I knew that we needed to do everything we could to prepare for the then "impending" revised English translation of the *Missale Romanum*. To that end, I created electronic source files that contained all of the texts for Mass that we publish in our worship resources: Entrance Chants, Opening Prayers, Prayers over the Gifts, Communion Chants, Prayers after Communion. My plan was that we would simply change the very few words in these songs and prayers precipitated by the revised translation of the original Latin when the translation was promulgated. I was proud of my work, feeling that I was contributing to the success of our company. One day I mentioned this approach to my friend Father Paul Turner. He simply replied, "Jerry, throw them all out; it looks like what we are going to end up with are significantly altered texts, mainly due to the new rules of translation." This was my first indication that what we were about to embark upon was not simply a slight adjustment; it seemed like it was going to be more like a major mid-course correction.

In the years during which the new translation was being prepared and bits and pieces were being submitted to the bishops of the United States, there really wasn't much that a music publisher could do, since we did not have the actual approved texts themselves. Several members of our WLP staff spent time at many national conferences, listening to presentations given by leaders of the International Commission on English in the Liturgy (ICEL), as well as the Bishops' Committee on Divine Worship (BCDW). We needed to do everything we could to get as much information as possible in order to be prepared for the time that the new translation would be approved.

June 23, 2008, proved to be the first pivotal date for us as a music publisher. On that date, Cardinal Francis Arinze, prefect of the Congregation for Divine Worship and the Discipline of the Sacraments, in a letter to Cardinal Francis George, president of the United States Conference of Catholic Bishops, stated the following:

> This Congregation for Divine Worship and the Discipline of the Sacraments is pleased to enclose the decree by which it has granted *recognitio* for the territory of your Conference of Bishops for the new English-language translation of significant parts of the *Ordo Missae* as found in the *Missale Romanum, editio typica tertia*, including most of those texts used in every celebration of Holy Mass.
>
> This Dicastery has no little satisfaction in arriving at this juncture. Nevertheless, the Congregation does not intend that these texts should be put into liturgical use immediately. Instead, the granting now of the *recognitio* to this crucial segment of *The Roman Missal* will provide time for the pastoral preparation of priests, deacons, and for appropriate catechesis of the lay faithful. It will likewise facilitate the devising of musical settings of the Mass, bearing in mind the criteria set forth in the Instruction, *Liturgiam Authenticam*, number 60, which requires that the musical settings of liturgical texts use only the actual approved texts and never be paraphrased.[10]

With this letter, and the soon-to-be-released texts from the Order of Mass, we swung into full gear. For a few years, we had—like most others with their "ear to the ground"—obtained copies of the Order of Mass that we were told were "very close" to what the final

---

10. Cf. *Congregatio de Culto Divino et Disciplina Sacramentorum*, Port. N. 1464/06/L; letter from Cardinal Francis Arinze to Cardinal Francis George, June 23, 2008.

translation would be. We even had some composers work with those translations. With Cardinal Arinze's letter and the new texts, we were able to begin to make some important decisions.

Throughout this time, I was busy giving workshops at events like the conventions of the National Association of Pastoral Musicians (NPM). I began to ask music directors and clergy members a simple question: "Do you think that, when we have the new English translation of the Mass, you will want to sing revised versions of the current musical settings of the Mass or do you think that you will want to sing newly commissioned settings?" At first, the majority of people said that they wanted revised versions of the current settings. I remember one person raising her hand and saying, "Please, please do not take away my *Mass of Creation*."

Like the other Catholic music publishing houses, we at WLP began to take a good look at our current musical settings of the Mass in an effort to decide which settings we wanted to revise. We survey our worship resource subscribers on an annual basis and have reliable information regarding which settings are well-liked and are sung regularly in parishes. Our company has been in existence for quite some time. Two of our "heritage" Masses—*People's Mass* and *Mass for Christian Unity*—both a part of the Catholic treasury since the years after the Second Vatican Council—were written by Jan Vermulst, who died in 1994. We decided that these two settings, popular among our subscribers and non-subscribers alike, needed to be revised. We commissioned the late Richard Proulx to revise these two settings, asking that he work in such a way that the melodic and harmonic structures of the original settings be maintained. We also chose several other popular settings and asked the still living composers to adapt their current settings to the newly translated text.

Some revisions were quite simple. Most composers had little problem with the Sanctus. There was only a small change in the first line, from "Lord, God of power and might" to "Lord God of hosts." Most settings could easily accommodate this slight change. The greatest challenge came with the Gloria and the newly translated Memorial Acclamations. Most of our composers had to return to the drawing board in order to compose new musical settings of the Gloria. For the most part, they felt that trying to retrofit the new text into the existing rhythmic, harmonic, and melodic structures was like trying to put the proverbial square peg into the round hole. Steven R. Janco's *Mass of Redemption*, one of WLP's most popular Mass settings, and J. Michael Joncas's *Sing Praise and Thanksgiving Mass* serve as examples of two settings where the Gloria has been thoroughly recomposed.

We gave careful thought to the commissioning of new musical settings. Our first concern was the parish itself. We know that there exists a great variety of musical resources in parishes across the country. In some places, there is no musician at all to lead the music and texts for Mass are sung without accompaniment. In others, there is an organist or pianist who leads the singing from the keyboard. Other places have a guitarist who leads the music. There are places with full choirs at one, two, or at every Mass. Some parishes have a variety of musical "forces" spread throughout their Mass schedule. There are parishes that have embraced chant almost completely. There are parishes where most Masses are in English and some where there are bilingual (English and Spanish) Masses, while other parishes are predominantly Spanish-speaking. We wanted to be consistent with our mission to serve the needs of the singing and praying Church. This meant that we necessarily had to begin with the actual experience of the people in parishes. To that end, we decided to commission new settings that would address this real experience.

In response to the variety of pastoral and musical situations in parishes, we took a multi-pronged approach. We commissioned a setting that is quite chant-like. It can be sung unaccompanied or with light supportive accompaniment. We also commissioned a new chant setting for the Gloria. From there, we moved to commissioning settings that could be used by the many contemporary ensembles whose primary instruments are keyboard, guitar, and C-instrument. We also commissioned a few settings that are scored for the full forces of SATB choir, organ, and brass. No matter which setting we commissioned and reviewed, there was one principle that drove our decision-making more than any other: the melody for the assembly had to support the newly translated text and had to be very accessible for the person in the pew.

As this process moved along, it became clearer and clearer to me that music—this gift of song—will play a key role in the "success", if you will, of the implementation of the newly translated texts. This was confirmed a few years ago when I attended a symposium focused on the newly translated texts. It was sponsored by the National Association of Pastoral Musicians. A group of approximately 150 musicians and pastors met together to talk about the issues that were beginning to be raised about the relationship between the newly translated texts and the music for those texts. It became clear that most were in agreement that music, indeed, would be a strong catalyst for the implementation of the new texts.

At WLP, once we had a few of the revised settings, as well as some of the new settings in hand, I decided to do some field testing. I gathered with a small group of music directors in the Archdiocese of Miami. First we sang the revised Gloria from Vermulst's *Mass for Christian Unity,* which had been reworked by Richard Proulx. The response was surprising. Several of the more "seasoned" music directors—for whom the original Gloria from this Mass was already a part of their "Catholic DNA"—complained that the setting seemed awkward and stilted. The younger directors—who had never sung the original—found the setting to move along quite naturally. This made me think about how these "retrofitted" settings were, or were not, going to work in a parish made up of more "seasoned" Catholics, as well as younger Catholics. One of the challenges in writing this essay is the fact that we really do not have a lived parish experience of the singing of these settings to analyze. It is very difficult to predict how the decisions made by the music publishers will actually help or hinder the implementation of the revised translations. It will be an interesting exercise to return to the essays in this book after the Church has had a long experience of praying and singing the texts.

At that Miami session, we also sang through a brand new through-composed chant setting of the Gloria, the *Gloria Simplex,* which Richard Proulx had composed for us. It flowed as naturally as any other chant setting of the Gloria I have ever sung or lead in parishes. No one stumbled over the new words. I came to the conclusion that it was the superb chant writing that made this setting "work" for those in the room. I began to become more and more convinced that good musical settings of the newly translated texts were going to be a real key in the success of their reception.

By the time I did that Miami session, ICEL had posted some of the proposed chant settings on their Web site, giving the publishers a special code to access these. I also brought these along with me.

This was to be my first singing of these settings with any group. We sang through the dialogues, the Gloria, the Sanctus, the Memorial Acclamations, and the Lamb of God. All agreed that the new chant settings were quite singable.

I decided to try out this kind of singing experiment at the next NPM convention, at which I had been invited to speak on the topic of the new translation. I polled the audience before the session, asking them whether or not they thought they would prefer revised musical settings or new musical settings. It was nearly an even split. Over the course of a year, it seemed that people were growing a bit more in favor of newly composed musical settings.

I brought the group of about 100 musicians through the same exercise that we did in Miami. After we sang through the ICEL chant setting of the Gloria, a priest who serves in Spanish-speaking parishes made a comment. He said that he found no problem with singing the newly translated English texts because they were now close—almost word for word—to the text in Spanish. I had known all along that the Spanish translation was closer to the original Latin than was our current English translation; this priest's experience drove that point home for all of us. When we sang through some of the revised musical settings, there were groans heard in the room. The "groaners" said that their hearts and voices couldn't easily move in the direction that the newly translated text was taking them because the music that had become ingrained in them seemed to pull them in another direction. This caused some to become irritated and part of the session was spent on complaining about the whole process, with questions raised such as, "Why do we have to change?" "Why is Rome insisting on this?" "Are you telling me that the prayers I have been praying and singing all these years are somehow deficient—what does this say about my own spiritual development? Is it somehow deficient?" There are other writers in this book whose task it is to address these questions. Musicians should take note, though, that these questions are the kinds of questions that will be asked of us when the new translation is implemented. And we better have answers at the ready. I am afraid that the answer, "Because the Vatican changed the rules of translation" simply will not fly in our parishes. We need to be able to explain clearly why the translation rules did change.

Up to this point, every one of my experiences sharing the new musical settings was with a group of professional musicians or clergy. Then I was invited to present an evening as part of a parish mission at a parish in the Archdiocese of Chicago. That parish's pastoral staff members had met earlier in the year to determine how best a parish mission could address the current needs and concerns of the parishioners. The staff felt that it wasn't too early to begin to catechize their people on the subject of the new English translation.

As I prepared my session for that parish mission, there was a part of me that felt like I was a lamb sent among the wolves. For the past year, I have been posting comments on my blog: *Gotta Sing, Gotta Pray.*[11] On that blog, I offer reflection on liturgy, music, and Christian initiation, as well as my own reflections on issues facing the Church today. In November of 2009, I began to devote my remarks on Tuesdays and Thursdays to the new translation. The morning after I offered the evening at the parish mission, I reflected on my experience on my blog. Even though the reflection is long, I have decided to include it here in its entirety, since it represented, for me, a real sense of where people in the pews were with regard to the new translation. I also offer it here, as a kind of pastoral response to the musical settings. I offer it also in the hopes that it will help pastoral, liturgical, and musical leaders during times of catechesis and communication in the years to come.

"On Tuesday night of this week, I was invited to present an evening of reflection at St. Mary Parish in Buffalo Grove, Illinois, about the upcoming new English translation of the *Missale Romanum.* There was a nice crowd in attendance, probably between 250 and 300. I would say that the majority of people who came were over 50 years of age.

"I decided not to begin the evening by diving right into the discussion about the new translation. Instead, I laid the groundwork for an exploration of the meaning of the Mass. My aim was to bring the folks to a deeper appreciation that when we celebrate the Eucharist, we proclaim the Death of the Lord. At Mass, I shared, we are drawn into the celebration of the Paschal Mystery and, at every Mass, God works a miracle of transformation in the hearts of all believers. Using stories about the illness and death of my sister nine years ago and the

---

11. Jerry Galipeau's blog, *Gotta Sing, Gotta Pray*, can be accessed at this Web site: http://gottasinggottapray.blogspot.com/.

more recent diagnosis of cancer for another one of my sisters, I shared with the people at Saint Mary how these profound moments in my life were able to be transformed and put into a faith perspective through God's grace, coupled with my own engagement at Sunday Mass. My conclusion was this: even though the texts of the Mass will change, the Mass will not change. Whatever language or translation we use, the fact is that bread and wine become the Body and Blood of Christ, and we become transformed once again into Christ's body for the life of the world.

"Once I laid this foundation, I moved into a simple walk through of how we have arrived at this point. Here are the points I covered:

1. There was one set of rules (principles of "dynamic equivalence") that were in place when the *Missale Romanum* was translated following the Second Vatican Council. What we eventually received as English-speakers (after provisional translations) is what we have been praying now for 40 or so years. I explained the principles of "dynamic equivalence" and felt that those in attendance were right there with me.

2. I then spoke about the third typical edition of the *Missale Romanum* promulgated by Pope John Paul II in the Jubilee year of 2000, an edition that added more texts (saints days, various needs, etc.). I told them that, with this new Missal, the task of translating it into the various languages needed to take place.

3. I then described that the rules of translation changed in 2001, with the Vatican's publication of *Liturgiam authenticam*. I quoted the document, citing paragraph 20:

> While it is permissible to arrange the wording, the syntax and the style in such a way as to prepare a flowing vernacular text suitable to the rhythm of popular prayer, the original text insofar as possible, must be translated integrally and in the most exact manner, without omissions or additions in terms of their content, and without paraphrases or glosses.[12]

I explained that the new rules were intended to bring the English translation, which many felt had been too rushed, into more consonance with the Latin text. The result, I told them, was that the work

---

12. *Liturgiam authenticam*, 20.

of ICEL needed to be closely guided by the new principles of "formal equivalence."

4. We then prayed the new translation of the Gloria together. I simply used the new translation of the first line of the Gloria (*Glória in excélsis Deo / et in terra pax homínibus bonae voluntátis*), showing them how the new translation ("Glory to God in the highest, / and on earth peace to people of good will") is much closer to the original Latin than our current translation ("Glory to God in the highest, / and peace to his people on earth)." I thought this would illustrate in rather simple and straightforward fashion how newly applied rules changed the way the text was translated.

5. We then sang through some settings of the newly translated Gloria, the Sanctus, and one of the Memorial Acclamations. People joined in wholeheartedly.

"Then I asked for questions, reactions, comments, and concerns. Here is what happened. Please understand that these are not exact quotes, but my best recollections.

"The first person to speak said something like this, "Well, Jerry, I came tonight with all kinds of anxieties and concerns about this issue. But I think that if our pastors explained all of this to everyone in parishes just like you just did, so much anxiety and fear will be alleviated. Thank you for this simple explanation."

"Well, dear readers, I was feeling great!

"Then a man in the choir said something like this: "When I was younger and the Mass was in Latin, I did lots of traveling throughout the world, and I had my Missal with me, with the English on one side and the Latin on the other. Wherever I went in the world, when the Mass was celebrated in Latin, I was able to follow along in English. So, I think it would be best if maybe we returned to the Latin."

"I commented that it has been strongly suggested (in several recent documents) that all Catholics should be able to pray the Gloria, Creed, Sanctus, Lord's Prayer, and Lamb of God in Latin, so that at international gatherings of people who speak many different languages, there could be a common liturgical language that would draw all into the celebration.

"I looked out and asked if there were any more questions. An elderly man raised his hand, stood up, and simply said, "Why is all of this happening?" I calmly explained that the first 45 minutes of the presentation had already really answered that question; I then did a brief recap of what I had said earlier. He remained standing, raised his hand again and said, "Why is all of this happening?"

"There was, to be sure, some tension growing in the church.

"Then a woman raised her hand. In her other hand she held a stack of papers. She said that she had downloaded the newly translated texts and had them in her hand. She said that she just didn't understand why this was all happening. She commented that, as an intelligent woman, when she read through these texts she wondered why certain words were included, words that she did not even know the meaning of, words like "ineffable." She then mentioned the Web site "What If We Just Said Wait." She said that she thought that with the new translation, people would leave the Church. Her husband, who was seated next to her said something like this: "I have always worked under the adage, 'If it ain't broke, don't fix it.' I don't understand why these changes are needed."

"I explained that I felt that the real question, the root of all these questions, did not necessarily have that much to do with 'Why the changes in texts?' The core question really is 'Why did the translation rules change?' And to be honest, I believe that this is the question. I explained again that we had to look to the pontificate of John Paul II and try to put it all in context. The Pope and others were keenly concerned with so-called 'liturgical abuses' that they perceived were occurring all over the world; things like priests adding their own words to the Mass texts; priests using experimental prayers; priests experimenting with 'inclusive language'; liturgy committees adding all kinds of strange things to the celebration of liturgy; a feeling that the sacred was being eroded because of these so-called 'abuses.' The Pope's reaction was to tighten liturgical control in a number of areas. I did not go into detail, but explained that *Liturgiam authenticam* was the Vatican's definitive statement, set into context, that changed the rules of translation, so that the vernacular languages would be in much tighter and closer conformity to the original Latin. This was consistent with the overall tightening of liturgical control; the issuance of liturgical directives that would directly address the so-called 'abuses' during the pontificate of John Paul II. (As I was speaking, I was aware that a one-night session at a parish mission could not adequately address every issue. I feared that I was leaving the people with more confusion than clarity.)

"A young woman, who I believe was the parish's youth minister, stood up and said that we really need to see this whole thing as the will of the Lord, and that if we accept the will of God, God will act in all of this.

"The pastor then asked me to comment on the ICEL chants. I told everyone that a group of chant scholars had created chants that the entire English-speaking world could use to sing the Mass. I said that I thought it was a great idea, since the entire English-speaking Catholic world would have at least one common setting of the sung Mass in English. The man in the choir said that we should be singing these in Latin. Someone near the front shouted loudly, 'We are not chanters for goodness sakes; we are Americans!' In response, I immediately intoned the commonly used chant setting of the Lord's Prayer and everyone sang it. When we finished, the person said, 'Well, maybe we Americans can chant one.'

"A priest in residence at the parish (who has traveled quite extensively internationally) voiced his own concerns about the image of God embedded and expressed in the newly translated texts. He said that he was very concerned about what he perceived as a "turning back" with the new texts.

"Dear readers of *Gotta Sing, Gotta Pray*, all I can say is that I found the evening to be fascinating and exhilarating. I told the people that I thought that when the new texts are promulgated for use, there will be a percentage of people who will be angry. Some will reject the new texts and, sadly, some may even be driven away. I said that there would also be a percentage of people who will accept the texts gladly, with little concern. I then said that I thought that the vast majority of Catholics would be jolted by the new texts. And that jolt would provide an opportunity for exactly what we were doing that evening. I told them that I hoped that this jolt would provide the opportunity not to wallow around in anger, but to ask questions about the translation and, ultimately ask questions about the meaning of the Mass; ask questions about what God is doing as we celebrate the liturgy.

"As I write this essay, the staff at WLP is busy working on the editing, engraving, recording, and production of new and revised musical settings for the new translation. Frankly, the years ahead present a large unknown for all of us. Our hope, of course, is that the work we do as a music publisher will help the people of God through this time of transition."[13]

CONCLUSION

On April 28, 2010, shortly before the *recognitio* for the revised translation was granted, Pope Benedict XVI addressed the members of the Vox Clara committee. One paragraph of that brief address stands out:

> A new task will then present itself, one which falls outside the direct competence of Vox Clara, but which in one way or another will involve all of you—the task of preparing for the reception of the new translation by clergy and lay faithful. Many will find it hard to adjust to unfamiliar texts after nearly 40 years of continuous use of the previous translation. The change will need to be introduced with due sensitivity, and the opportunity for catechesis that it presents will need to be firmly grasped. I pray that in this way any risk of confusion or bewilderment will be averted, and the change will serve instead as a springboard for a renewal and a deepening of Eucharistic devotion all over the English-speaking world.[14]

Pope Benedict's words—deeply pastoral in nature—underscore the challenges faced by the Church in the coming years. Obviously, I believe that music will greatly assist the implementation of the newly translated texts. *Sing to the Lord* draws our attention to the song that is the liturgy: "The primordial song of the liturgy is the canticle of victory over sin and death."[15]

Music—the gift of song—has the capacity to draw us more deeply into the Paschal Mystery than words alone. As we begin to become accustomed to new words, it is my hope that this primordial song draws all those at the Liturgy into a deeper experience of God's ongoing work of salvation through the Death and Resurrection of Christ.

---

13. From *Gotta Sing, Gotta Pray*; originally posted on Thursday, March 4, 2010.

14. Address of Pope Benedict XVI to the members of the Vox Clara committee, April 28, 2010.

15. STL, 7.

Contributors

Francis Cardinal George, OMI, is the first native Chicagoan to be named Archbishop of Chicago. Installed in May 1997, the Cardinal arrived by way of the west coast, where he had spent less than a year as Archbishop of Portland, Oregon, and five years as Bishop of Yakima, Washington. He is the thirteenth Ordinary, and sixth Cardinal, for the Archdiocese of Chicago since its establishment in 1843.

Raised on Chicago's northwest side, Cardinal George is a member of the Missionary Oblates of Mary Immaculate. He shepherds the Archdiocese's 2.3 million Catholics. In 2007, he was elected to a three-year term as President of the United States Conference of Catholic Bishops. Cardinal George holds doctoral degrees in both American Philosophy (Tulane University) and Ecclesiology (the Pontifical Urban University). He is fluent in Italian and French and conversant in both Spanish and German.

Locally, he leads his diverse flock with an energy that belies his age. He is the first Cardinal Archbishop to visit all of the Archdiocese's 363 parishes, and to communicate digitally, electronically, and in the three primary languages of the Archdiocese of Chicago: English, Spanish, and Polish. He even has his own blog! Internationally, he serves as a member of the Congregation for Evangelization of Peoples, the Pontifical Council for Culture, *Cor Unum*, the Congregation for Oriental Churches, and the Roman Congregation for Divine Worship and the Discipline of the Sacraments, as well as the Vox Clara Subcommittee of this Congregation.

For over ten years Cardinal George served as the USCCB representative to the Episcopal Board of the International Commission on English in the Liturgy. He is the founding Archbishop of the Liturgical Institute at Mundelein Seminary. He is a much sought after speaker and author, both locally and internationally. We are proud to have him as our Ordinary here in Chicago.

Monsignor Andrew R. Wadsworth, MA, MA, GTCL, LTCL, LRAM, is a priest of the Archdiocese of Westminster in the United Kingdom.

After graduate studies in music at Trinity College London and the
Royal Academy of Music, he trained as a répétiteur with English
National Opera. He also holds graduate degrees in Italian and
Theology. Ordained in 1990, he has had a wide range of pastoral
experience in parishes, schools, universities, and hospitals. A former
professor of Ecclesiastical Latin and New Testament Greek at the
Westminster Diocesan Seminary, he has also taught Italian at the
college and university levels. As a musician, he has performed,
recorded, and broadcasted extensively. In recent years, Monsignor
Wadsworth has directed a number of seminars for priests concentrat-
ing on the *ars celebrandi*. He was appointed Executive Director of
ICEL in the fall of 2009.

Monsignor Anthony F. Sherman, STD, was the Executive Director
of the USCCB Secretariat of Divine Worship. A priest of the Diocese
of Brooklyn, he holds a master's in theology and a doctorate in sacred
theology, with a major in liturgy, from the University of Innsbruck,
Austria. He was an adjunct professor of liturgy at Immaculate
Conception Seminary, Huntington, Long Island for more than
twenty years. As former director of the diocesan liturgy office and as
an associate pastor and pastor of St. Matthias Parish, Ridgewood,
New York, he has dealt with both the academic and pastoral aspects
of liturgy. Monsignor Sherman is a member of the North American
Academy of Liturgy and the Catholic Academy of Liturgy. He has
published on the subjects of death and dying, Baptism preparation,
and the *Rite of Christian Initiation of Adults*.

Reverend Robert L. Tuzik, STL, PHD, is a priest of the Archdiocese
of Chicago. He holds an STL from the University of St. Mary of the
Lake and a PHD in liturgical studies from the University of Notre
Dame. He has been an associate pastor of five parishes in Chicago
and is currently special projects coordinator for the Office of Divine
Worship of the Archdiocese of Chicago. He also serves as liturgical
consultant to His Eminence, Cardinal Francis George, OMI. He has
served as special consultant to ICEL and the BCL (now BCDW) and
is a member of the Society for Catholic Liturgy and Region VII of
the FDLC. He has served as adjunct professor of liturgy at the
University of St. Mary of the Lake and as a lecturer at Loyola

University of Chicago. He has published numerous articles in *Pastoral Liturgy, Liturgical Ministry, Modern Liturgy, Assembly,* and *Antiphon* and is the author of *Reynold Hillenbrand: The Reform of the Catholic Liturgy and the Call to Social Action.*

Reverend Paul Turner, STL, is pastor of St. Munchin parish in Cameron, Missouri, and its mission, St. Aloysius in Maysville. A priest of the diocese of Kansas City–St. Joseph, he holds a doctorate in sacred theology from Sant' Anselmo in Rome.

His books include *The Catechumenate Answer Book* (Resource Publications, 2000), *Your Child's Baptism* (Liturgy Training Publications, 1999), *The Hallelujah Highway: A History of the Catechumenate* (Liturgy Training Publications, 2000), *The Catholic Wedding Answer Book* (Resource Publications, 2001), *Let Us Pray: A Guide to the Rubrics of Sunday Mass* (Liturgical Press, 2006), *When Other Christians Become Catholic* (Liturgical Press, 2007), *Celebrating Initiation: A Guide For Priests* (World Library Publications, 2008), *Understanding the Revised Mass Texts, Second Edition* (Liturgy Training Publications, 2010), and *At the Supper of the Lamb: A Pastoral and Theological Commentary on the Mass* (Liturgy Training Publications, 2011). He writes "Bulletin Inserts" for *Ministry and Liturgy.*

He is a former President of the North American Academy of Liturgy and a team member for the North American Forum on the Catechumenate. He serves as a facilitator for the International Commission on English in the Liturgy.

Monsignor James P. Moroney, STB, STL, a priest of the Diocese of Worcester for the past 29 years, is rector of Saint Paul's Cathedral and serves as a member of the faculty of Saint John's Seminary in Boston. He pursued graduate studies at the Pontifical Gregorian University, the Pontifical Liturgy Institute at Saint Anselmo's, and the Catholic University of America. A past chairman of the Federation of Diocesan Liturgical Commissions, Monsignor Moroney was Executive Director of the USCCB Secretariat for the Liturgy from 1996–2007. Pope John Paul II appointed him as the fourth American to serve as a consultor to the Congregation for Divine Worship and the Discipline of the Sacraments since the Second Vatican Council. Pope Benedict XVI has reappointed him as a consultor to that Congregation, which he also serves as Executive Secretary to the Vox Clara Committee. Monsignor Moroney is a frequent lecturer on liturgical matters, having addressed more than 17,000 priests and deacons in recent years at the invitation of close to one hundred bishops.

Reverend Ronald T. Kunkel, STB, STL, STD (candidate), was ordained a priest of the Archdiocese of Chicago in May of 2000. He holds degrees from the University of Notre Dame, the Pontifical Gregorian University, and the Pontifical Athenaeum of Saint Anselm. Father Kunkel is a candidate for a Doctorate in Sacred Theology at the University of Saint Mary of the Lake.

After completing an advanced degree in sacramental theology in Rome, Father Kunkel was appointed Associate Pastor at Saint Peter Parish, Skokie, Illinois, in July of 2001. From January 2002 through June 2005, he served as Associate Pastor and Director of Liturgy at Holy Name Cathedral, Chicago.

Currently, Father Kunkel is a member of the faculty at Mundelein Seminary, teaching courses in the areas of liturgy, sacraments, and Christian anthropology. He also provides sacramental assistance at Saint Mary Parish, Lake Forest.

Father Kunkel is a member of the Society for Catholic Liturgy and the Fellowship of Catholic Scholars, and was a founding member of the board of directors for the Illinois Catholic Prayer Breakfast.

Reverend Ronald J. Lewinski, STL, ordained a priest in 1972 for the Archdiocese of Chicago, is pastor of St. Mary of the Annunciation Parish in Mundelein, Illinois, and also serves as a Dean (Vicar Forane) for the Archdiocese. He is a former Director of the Office for Divine Worship for the Archdiocese of Chicago and has taught Liturgy and Sacraments at the Mundelein Seminary and Loyola University. Father Lewinski is a respected author and a frequent speaker on Liturgy, Christian Initiation, and Pastoral Life across the United States of America, Canada, Australia, Germany, South Africa, and South East Asia. He is best known for his work with the *Rite of Christian Initiation of Adults*. He is the author of *Welcoming the New Catholic*, *A Guide for Sponsors*, and *Making Parish Policy*. Father Lewinski has served as an advisory board member for Notre Dame's Center for Liturgy and on ad hoc commissions for the United States Bishops' Committee on the Liturgy and continues to serve as the President of the ACTA Foundation. He is recognized as someone who effectively blends together liturgy, sacramental theology, and pastoral life.

Reverend James Presta, STD, ordained in 1986 for the Archdiocese of Chicago, received a BS in Psychology and Theology from Loyola University; and an MDIV (*magna cum laude*) and STL from the University of St. Mary of the Lake / Mundelein Seminary. In 2005, he earned a doctoral degree, STD (*magna cum laude*), at the International Marian Research Institute, which is affiliated with the Pontifical University Marianum in Rome.

After ordination, Father Presta served as a parish priest at St. Christopher in Midlothian (1986–1993) and at Queen of Martyrs in Evergreen Park (1993–1996). In May 1996, His Eminence Joseph Cardinal Bernardin appointed him the seventh Rector-President of the college seminary of the Archdiocese of Chicago, St. Joseph College Seminary, located on the campus of Loyola University at the lakeshore. He was also Director of the Tuite Program at St. Joseph. Father Presta served on the Board of Advisors of Mundelein Seminary, was the Executive Secretary of the Board of Advisors of St. Joseph College Seminary, served as Chairman of the Priest Placement Board of the Archdiocese of Chicago, and was a member of the Executive Committee of the Presbyteral Council of the Archdiocese.

Father Presta's academic affiliations include the National Association of College Seminaries (NACS), the Fellowship of Catholic Scholars, and the Mariological Society of America. His current work and research is in Mariology and he has given workshops, days of recollection, and parish missions on the Blessed Virgin Mary.

The National Association of College Seminaries honored Father Presta, in June of 2010, with the St. John Vianney Award for his outstanding service to the Church in the formation of college seminarians.

Father Presta concluded his term as Rector-President of St. Joseph College Seminary on June 30, 2010. His Eminence Francis Cardinal George appointed Father Presta as a full-time faculty member at the University of St. Mary of the Lake / Mundelein Seminary. He is the Associate Dean of Formation and an Assistant Professor in the Department of Systematic Theology.

Jerry Galipeau, DMIN, is Associate Publisher at World Library Publications, the music and liturgy division of J. S. Paluch Company in Franklin Park, Illinois. A writer, composer, and former parish liturgist and musician, Jerry presents keynotes and workshops throughout North America on initiation, liturgical spirituality, ritual music, and evangelization. He earned the Doctor of Ministry with a concentration in liturgical studies from Catholic Theological Union at Chicago in 1999. His popular blog, "Gotta Sing, Gotta Pray" focuses on music, liturgy, and Christian initiation: gottasinggottapray. blogspot.com.